PRACTICAL PRINTMAKING

PRACTICAL PRINTMAKING

CHARTWELL BOOKS, INC.

First published in the United States by
Chartwell Books Inc.
A division of Book Sales Inc.
110 Enterprise Avenue
Secaucas, New Jersey 07094

ISBN 0-89009-536-1

Produced by Winchmore Publishing Services
Limited,
40 Triton Square
London NW1.
England

House Editor: Sue Butterworth
Designed by: Laurence Bradbury

Printed in Hong Kong

CONTENTS

INTRODUCTION

Like an apothecary's shop, was how a print workshop was once described. Jars of pigment, inks, paper, peculiar instruments, and large interesting machinery.

An established print studio with its smells and noises, creates an atmosphere which ranges from the tranquility of a country clock maker to the hustle and bustle of the engine sheds in Crewe! All have in common an air of excitement and discovery.

There are several ways in which people can become involved in printmaking; setting up with modest equipment at home, renting space in a print workshop, taking evening or part time classes, and by joining a full time course in an art school. Printmaking enables people involved in all aspects of Art and Design to explore new avenues, everyone it seems has a desire to go 'into print' in one form or another and for the serious student, doing is more constructive and exciting than being told about it.

Although there is an established method and procedure for each process there is always room for individual innovation, making use of textures and materials and exploiting the opportunities of change; in the etching section of this book the writer 'suggests' a method of working, as each individual soon discovers a personal approach to each process.

Printmaking has survived the aesthetic uncertainties of the past twenty years, possibly because of the technical demands and the need to have a full working knowledge of the process which lead to more concentrated images. One thing is certain – it will always have a magical quality, for when the process is complete you have a set of unique images.

This book will appeal to all those who are interested in printmaking, from the adventurous amateur to art students, professional printmakers and professional artists and designers. It covers as much ground as possible with good step by step photographs and is a sound guide to the practice of printmaking.

Robin Bagilhole

Same Again Mr. O'Malevitch.
Handcut, fillers and photostencil screenprint
27″ × 27″
Robin Bagilhole.

LITHOGRAPHY

GENERAL PRINCIPLES

LITHOGRAPHY IS A planographic printing process – the printing and non-printing areas lie in the same plane. With intaglio or letterpress the image is either recessed or raised from the background. The natural antipathy between grease and water is the fundamental principle of lithography so the first step in lithography is to obtain a surface on which deposited grease will be retained.

Whilst stone is the traditional lithographic surface, today the metal lithographic plate is more widely used. In fact, commercially, stone is never used so most workshops and art schools are geared primarily to plate and photo-plate lithography. Although both plastics and paper have been explored as possible lithographic surfaces, neither can sufficiently withstand the rigours of the printing process.

Grease retention is only effective on two metals, zinc and aluminium, and is possible because these metals can adsorb grease and more especially gum arabic the hygroscopic quality of which attracts water and so repels grease from the undrawn areas of a plate.

Adsorption is a complex physio-chemical phenomenon that manifests itself as a clinging bond between certain substances and for this union to work successfully on metal, the plate must be 'grained'. Graining approximately trebles the surface area of a plate allowing the plate to retain water more readily as well as allowing more extensive adsorption.

Specially prepared, high grease content, inks are used to draw the image on the grained metal. The printing inks also are greasy and are eventually attracted to the adsorbed grease left by the drawn image. However, to treat the undrawn areas in such a way as to repel grease, the plate must be sponged down with a solution of gum arabic. This bonds by clinging in the grain of all parts of the plate not covered by drawing grease, so stabilising the drawing.

In the final stage of processing it is necessary to replace the drawn grease with fluid printing ink and this stage is referred to as 'washing out'. Turpentine is used to 'wash out' the image, taking away the drawing pigment and leaving the fine, clinging grease residue. The residue is built up by a thin layer of extra grease, asphaltum, to make a stronger more even layer which will readily accept printing ink. All that remains is to rinse the plate in cold water to remove excess gum and asphaltum and the plate is ready to 'roll up' and print.

DEVELOPMENT

It took approximately one hundred years from the discovery of lithography by the German engraver Aloys Senefelder (1771–1834) in 1796 for zinc and aluminium plates to be successfully developed and used. It was also during the 1890s that lithography gathered impetus in France, gaining direction through a small number of artists drawn to the medium by the possibilities available.

The wide scope for linear and tonal drawing allied to the possibilities in the use of colour, made lithography a natural autographic medium for artists. The most influential of these artists was probably Toulouse Lautrec who elevated colour printing to a creative rather than reproductive art and later Picasso who extended the range of autographic image-making techniques with his continuously imaginative approach to different lithographic surfaces.

The technology quickly developed from the turn of the century and the discovery of offset printing in 1905 brought zinc and aluminium plates into use more extensively.

When he gets bored thinking about things, my cat sometimes plays the piano.
Lithograph/silk-screen 40″ × 31″
Len Gray.

LITHOGRAPHY

PRINTING WORKSHOPS

The expense of equipment or lack of space means that many artists find that working with or in a professional studio workshop is the best solution to exploiting the medium and realising a complete final image. Here the printer will cope with any technical problems that arise, working through the proofing stages to the *bon a tirer* and finally through the edition.

The 'rapport' between artist and printer that enabled so many imaginative ideas by painters such as Munch, Bonnard, Picasso to be realised owed much to Parisian printers like Clot, Ancourt and Mourlot. This relationship is just as important nowadays for with the advances in technology, the average artist wishing to utilise new developments in the medium can be blinded by the sheer complexity of process without a skilled specialist printer to help. Thus, more recent lithographs by the sculptor Henry Moore owe much to the technical expertise of Stanley Jones at Curwen Press for many of these images were arrived at through complex (photo-transfer) diazo drawing methods.

STUDIO EQUIPMENT

For any artist interested enough to have their own studio, a large well-lit room with a strong load-bearing floor to take the weight of the press is essential. The room must be free from damp as both paper and plates will otherwise suffer and although it is a great advantage to have natural light, a cool even working temperature is most important. Running water and electricity are, of course, essential.

In the layout it is helpful if all work surfaces are approximately the same height and are well-constructed. For ease of use, the press, inking slab and hanging racks for print drying should be kept close together while the graining sink should, if possible, have access to daylight or fluorescent light. In a basement or where daylight is poor, a good mix of fluorescent and ordinary incandescent bulbs gives a balanced light.

The processing sink
The processing sink (sometimes called the graining sink) is a very important piece of equipment used widely throughout the plate preparation stages. The sink must be approximately one metre (1·09 yd) square and 15 cm (6 in) in depth and placed about 90 cm (35·5 in) from the ground. Ideally it should be lined with an epoxy resin or pre-formed plastic lining. It must contain both a drainage hole and a removable wooden 'duck board' to support the plate. A flexible hose with a shower nozzle attached is most useful and a waste trap should be fitted under the sink.

Print drying racks
Ample drying facilities for wet prints are essential.
(1) The Ballrack – probably the most commonly used rack it can be strung on a pulley to enable prints to be hoisted out of the way to dry or it can be fixed rigidly out from the wall. These racks hold prints vertically by marble pressure at the top corners of the paper.
(2) Steel and wire racks – these useful racks hold the prints one above the other, horizontally, on wire and steel shelves. The units are normally on castors and each shelf is sprung at the back for easy loading. Many prints can be dried this way without fear of marking the paper.

Plate racks
Fresh plates must be stored in a dry place, ideally a drawer, interleaved with acid free tissue and kept well wrapped. This prevents oxidation from

Plate racks and ballracks.

Nap rollers (top and bottom) and glazed leather roller (middle) stored in an easy and convenient way.

moisture in the atmosphere or contamination by airborne grease. Once processed or proved plates can have a small hole punched in one corner so they can be hung from hooks between printings.

Roller racks
Rollers are best stored in racks either vertically or horizontally. Both methods are satisfactory provided the roller is held by its handles and nothing makes contact with the roller surface. A wooden box with semi-circular notches to take the handles is perfectly adequate for horizontal storage.

Lithographic rollers
Two types of roller are used in lithography.
(1) Nap rollers with an absorbent calf skin covering used primarily in conjunction with the non-drying black to prove the plate.
(2) Glazed leather or composition rollers which have a non-absorbent surface and are used in colour printing.

For most work a 30·5 cm (12 in) or 38 cm (15 in) roller will be adequate and one of each type of roller is necessary. Although rollers are expensive, with care they can last a lifetime. Loose leather hand grips are most important for all rollers as these permit the roller handles to rotate freely while inking up. A further roller that can be most useful is a small composition roller or 'brayer'.

(1) Nap rollers
Both nap and glazed rollers are made to the same pattern: a wooden stock is covered by several layers of felt or flannelette which is finally covered in calf skin. Thick draw-string threaded through holes at each end is then pulled tight and knotted, holding the calf skin in place over both ends of the roller.

New leather on a nap roller must be conditioned properly to keep it soft and to remove loose nap. The procedure is as follows:
(a) Russian tallow, olive oil or castor oil is rubbed into the surface of the roller and allowed to penetrate. Several applications are necessary over a period of four or five days. The roller must be kept free from dust and petroleum based oils should not be used as they harden leather.

LITHOGRAPHY

Above: *It's amazing what they can do for you
these days.*
Hand-drawn lithograph 41″ × 33″
John Ross.

Right: *The Wickwood.*
Hand-drawn lithograph 20″ × 30″
Randal Cooke.

(b) For several days the roller is rolled up in strong litho varnish and scraped each time carefully with a palette knife. The varnish helps clear the nap of loose material and raises the texture of the skin. It is important that the varnish is not allowed to dry out in the roller.

(c) The roller is charged with non-drying rolling up black and, as at the varnish stage, it is rolled up and scraped down for about a week.

The roller should now have a velvety texture and be 'cured' although for a further month it will probably continue to shed some nap. It is sufficient to scrape the roller after use now with a palette knife although, at least once a month, the roller should be covered with pure turpentine and vigorously brushed with a small scrubbing brush to bring up the pile. When the roller is scraped, the edge of the palette knife must be carefully drawn up the length of the roller and once the ink is wiped off the knife, the roller is turned slightly and the procedure repeated until the whole roller has been scraped. This is most important to do immediately if a dark colour has been used to avoid any matting and hardening of the nap due to drying ink.

Cleaning the roller nap by careful scraping so as to bring up the nap.

(2) Glazed rollers

Although largely supplanted by rubber or composition rollers, glazed rollers are easy to convert from old nap rollers and once surfaced are extremely hard wearing. There are two methods of conversion:

(a) Roll up the roller with a good drying ink (one of the 'umbers') and while it is still wet, roll the colour out of the roller on to a damp stone which will flatten and glaze the roller surface. This should be continued for a few days, allowing the glazed ink to dry between each session until a good layer of ink, impervious to any penetration by other colours, is formed.

(b) Roll up the roller with a thin coat of *Terebine* (a derivitive of genuine turpentine). Once dry, smooth the roller with a fine grade 'wet or dry' paper and wipe down with paraffin. Terebine will ensure that much of the suppleness of the original leather is retained.

Should it be necessary on a leather roller to re-do a glaze or clear the nap of dried ink, a mixture of pure turpentine and carbolic acid should be used. Gloves *must* be worn when using carbolic acid and care should be taken to avoid splashing the skin. This mix (approximately seven drops of carbolic to twenty millilitres of turpentine) should be generously applied to the roller and after a few moments the glaze or dried ink will soften so assisting removal from the roller by careful scraping.

(3) Rubber or composition rollers

These rollers have an advantage over the glazed leather type in that they are formed of a solid casing of composition or rubber made around an aluminium spindle. This eliminates any slight unevenness that the glazed rollers have due to a leather joint along the length of each roller, although with careful rolling this is unlikely to manifest itself through an uneven ink layer. Gelatine rollers are best avoided as they can easily lose their shape or surface through either too much heat or the wrong solvent being accidentally applied. Most composition rollers should *not* be cleaned with pure turpentine and should be kept in racks to ensure the roller surface remains clean and protected.

Direct and offset presses

(1) Direct

The old direct flat bed presses are ideal for the artist/printer although you may have to search hard before finding a suitable one. These robust presses are rarely used now in commercial printing, tending to be superseded by fast offset machines and although new direct presses are available, they are expensive.

The word 'direct' refers to the method whereby paper is placed, before printing, directly on to the inked surface of the plate. A plate is mounted on a removable steel base to raise the level of the bed. Plate and printing paper are now covered with extra 'backing' sheets of paper, at least the size of the

Direct press.

Offset press.

printing paper to act as a cushioning and all are then covered with a sheet of metal (brass) or plastic called the 'tympan'. The bed and its load now has to be pushed under a scraper bar; a fixed leather covered length of boxwood lying across the middle of the press. Now, by operating a pressure lever the drive cylinder under the bed of the press is raised, forcing the bed and its load upwards until it is squeezed under the scraper bar. When the bed is wound or driven, if a motor is used, through the press, the scraper bar exerts an even pressure through the greased tympan to the paper and the plate. The image is now printed and it will be noticed that by the direct process it is reversed.

On these direct presses, great care must be taken with the scraper as it directly affects the quality of the print. The scraper is bolted into a fixed holder which is centre pivoted by a pressure adjusting screw and it is this screw which controls the degree of pressure applied to the print. New leathers for scrapers should be well soaked in water before being fitted to the boxwood so that the leather becomes taut along the length of wood as it dries. Tallow should be liberally applied to the leather to help the scraper move freely along the tympan when printing proceeds.

(2) Offset

An offset press will produce an image which is the replica of the one drawn on the plate. The plate is placed on the printing bed of the machine. The image is damped and inked by hand and the paper is placed in the grippers at the opposite end of the machine. The travelling blanket takes the ink from the plate and transfers it to the paper held ready by the grippers. The rolling nature of the transfer from plate to paper via the blanket is particularly suited to the use of fine grain anodised aluminium photo-plates or fine wash drawings from ordinary plates for the ink film is greatly reduced. Much greater 'pick-up' from the grain of the plate is achieved by using this offset 'rolling' action than is possible with the 'squeezing' action of the direct presses. However, greater variation to the thickness of the ink film is possible by direct printing.

PREPARING LITHOGRAPHIC PLATES

It is best to buy either the zinc or aluminium plate already grained and a good medium surface is 100 grain – graining ranges from 60 coarse to 220 very fine. Mechanical graining is essential for plates as, although not cheap, it ensures an even, sharp grain across the plate surface, very difficult to achieve by hand.

One graining will probably do for two or three different drawings on the plate if careful erasing and resensitising is done between each image. Regraining, however, is then necessary due to the wear on the grain from the resensitising 'counter-etch'. Despite an average gauge of ·064 cm (·025 in), plates will take many regrainings.

In Europe, zinc is readily available so is the most used surface for autographic drawing. The same can be said for aluminium in the USA. Zinc and aluminium are very different in their reaction to grease for zinc is water repellant and grease receptive (oleophilic) by nature and aluminium is receptive to water and grease repellant (hydrophilic). These qualities tend to cancel out each other when any assessment is made of the two metals: an image on aluminium, for example, is not liable to scum or 'fill in' as on zinc, but equally it is harder to hold fine areas of greasy drawing on aluminium. Generally speaking, this holding ability of drawing grease by zinc is preferable, particularly for any fine wash type drawings, than the opposite and provided the plate is correctly proved and carefully rolled up, 'scum' should not be a problem.

Before drawing on either of these surfaces commences, a very dilute counter-etch solution must be floated over the plate surface for it is essential that any invisible oxide coat or grease marks from storage or handling are removed to ensure that the drawing ink makes proper contact with the plate. For this specific counter-etch, commercially made 'Prepasol' is ideal as this nitric acid/potash alum formula, at a one part Prepasol to twenty parts water dilution, will clean the grain of either metal without wearing it down. The method is as follows:

Overleaf: Experimental marks on lithoplate showing the vast range of textures and washes that can be achieved.

A selection of lithographic drawing materials.

(a) Pour some of the 1/20 Prepasol on to a damp plate.
(b) With a rocking motion spread the solution over the whole plate.
(c) Wash the Prepasol off and repeat the process at least once.
(d) The counter-etch should be washed off and the plate dried by heater immediately to avoid any possibility of oxidation.

It is important to note that the Prepasol is used in a very weak solution at this stage and only a very slight discolouration of the plate should occur.

DRAWING MATERIALS & METHODS

Commercially manufactured forms of grease are available from lithographic stockists. All are black for visual convenience and all contain a high proportion of grease, soap or fatty substances. Although the drawing sticks are normally diluted with turpentine or water, remarkable qualities can be achieved using Methyl Ethyl Ketone (MEK) or benzine. Mixing different media such as gum, water, drawing ink and turpentine together can produce very rich textures and experimentation is worthwhile. Pure turpentine is preferable to white spirit in that its resinous, oily nature contains greater grease attracting properties.

Chinagraph pencil

Rubbing block

Charbonnel lithographic crayon

Liquid litho drawing ink
This is a ready prepared grease/water ink that needs to be well shaken before use. It can be further diluted with ordinary water but for a very fine wash, distilled water is preferable. A useful ink for pen drawing.

Lithographic crayons
Conté shaped crayons, they tend to be imported from either France or the USA and come in five grades. The American grading is from 00 very soft to 5 (Copal) and the French grading is the reverse.

Rubbing blocks
These are greasy blocks of ink made in three grades, soft, medium and hard. A block can be applied by rag or finger to give a very soft velvety effect or it can be applied to a piece of material and offset on to a plate via the press, thus transferring the cloth texture to the plate.

Drawing sticks
Perhaps the most versatile form of grease, they can make both a water or turpentine based drawing ink. The stick is rubbed down on a dry dish shaped surface such as a saucer and once a reasonable amount of ink has been rubbed out, either water or turpentine is added until the required consistency of ink is reached. It is relatively easy by adding either more pigment or water/turps to achieve a wide variety of tones.

Korn lithographic crayon

Lithographic reproducing pencils
Of most use when fine registration marks are needed for colour printing. They look very similar to ordinary pencils and indeed a hard H or 2H pencil will give as satisfactory a result. It is not advisable to use any pencils extensively on lithographic surfaces for they are less greasy than the chalks and inks and are consequently less predictable.

Other possible drawing substances
Apart from hard pencils, several other items will pick up lithographically among them are oil pastels, ball-point pens and chinagraph pencils. As different makes vary, some experimenting will have to be done to find the most successful brands; the same is true for any oils, soaps, etc. Carbon paper is particularly greasy by nature and may be used for producing fine line drawings by laying it face down on the plate: a drawing on paper can then be placed over the carbon and drawn through directly on to the plate.

French drawing stick

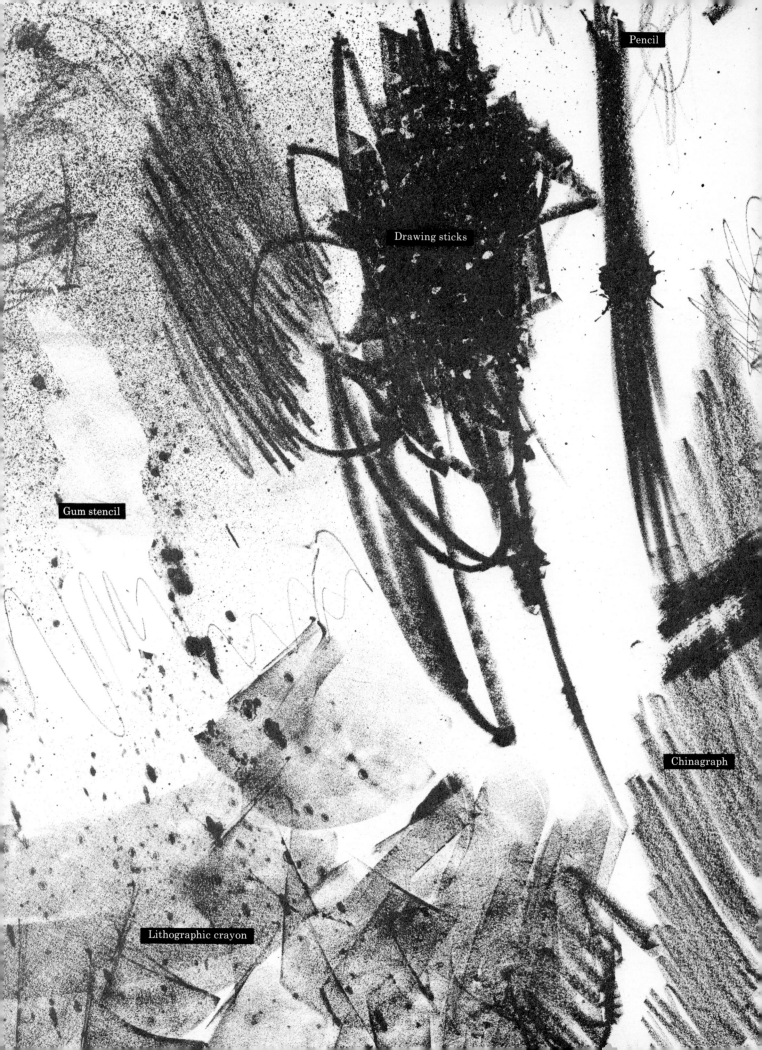

Drawing sticks

Pencil

Gum stencil

Chinagraph

Lithographic crayon

Carbon paper

Turps with brush

Pen and ink

Turps with dry brush

Gum with turps ink spattered

Water wash

LITHOGRAPHY

Non printing substances

Chalk, conté or charcoal will not pick up lithographically and are therefore useful for initial light drawing on a plate surface as an indication for later applications of grease. Chalk paper is also available, this reddish paper is used like the carbon paper though it does not print.

Gum arabic can also be used as a stop out for various areas of plate prior to drawing in grease. Once the gum has dried chalk work or turpentine-based ink can be used over the gum shapes and on to the plate as the gum will act as a stencil. As gum arabic is water soluble, it is important that any fluid ink is turpentine based for effective results.

Drawing implements

As the wide range of marks and textures possible in lithography will depend on the application of the grease, it is useful to have a good variety of brushes, pens etc. available. A toothbrush, for instances, can give an effective splatter quality, an airbrush a fine spray effect, and so on.

Methods
Transfer Lithographs

The use of transfer paper is sometimes preferable to drawing directly on a plate. Transfer paper has a water soluble gelatin/egg albumin coating applied evenly to one-side and it is on this side that the drawing is made with the lithographic chalks or inks. Once dry the drawing is transferred to the plate as follows:

(a) Damp a freshly prepared plate.
(b) Place the drawing face down on the damp surface.
(c) Apply at least five or six sheets of backing paper over the transfer paper and set a medium pressure on the press.
(d) Pass through the press twice.
(e) Remove the backing sheets, check that the paper is flat and lightly damp the back of the paper.
(f) Replace the backing sheets and pass through the press until the transfer paper takes on a semi-transparent look.
(g) Finally, peel the paper *carefully* off the plate.

At this stage, unless any additions or deletions are necessary, the transferred image should be dried and gummed.

One of the advantages of transfer paper is that apart from being very portable, it gives a great degree of flexibility to image making. It is possible to:

Collage or scrape back into the paper.
Add to or delete from the drawing after it has been transferred and before the plate has been processed.
Use thin layers of acrylic or gouache as 'stop outs' over greasy drawing on the paper.

The final image, when printed from a direct press, will also be the same way round as the initial drawing. Should a large wash type drawing be done on transfer paper, once transferred it will tend to be consistently stable because the ink is directly forced into the plate by the transfer. Major disadvantages of transfer paper are:

A certain loss of grease will take place in the transferring.
The water soluble film on some papers mean no water soluble inks can be used.

Unfortunately, few transfer papers are still made for, commercially, images are mostly transferred by the photo-litho method. This is a pity for the depth of tone and subtlety possible through the range of these papers and manifest in so many Picasso and Matisse images is difficult to achieve by photo-transferring without highly sophisticated machinery.

It is not, however, too difficult to make an adequate transfer paper using a thin layer of gum arabic sprayed on a smooth cartridge paper. Commercial gummed paper in sheets can also be satisfactorily used and is easily available. The one commercially made transfer paper available in this country is produced by the French firm of Charbonnel.

Lightly dampening the back of the paper before passing through the press and carefully removing the paper from the plate.

Other forms of transfer

(1) Photo-transfers

Images from newspapers, provided they are freshly printed can also be put down on a plate using a similar method to transferring. Instead of water, however, 'screenwash' or benzine should be brushed on the back and burnished through the reverse until the image is transferred. The plate is then gummed up.

(2) Printed image transfers

This is occasionally necessary when an edition is to be pulled from an unstable plate. The transfer is made from one plate to another. German 'Everdamp' a light brown transferring paper is made especially for this purpose and it is kept in a moistened state in an airtight container. The procedure is as follows:

(a) The plate is rolled up with a mixture of three parts rolling up black to one part retransfer ink.

(b) A print is taken on to the Everdamp.

(c) Provided a good image has come off on to the Everdamp, place it face down on a fresh plate.

(d) Cover with five or six sheets of backing paper and run through the press at least twice.

(e) Carefully peel off the Everdamp, dust with French chalk and gum up.

(3) Indirect drawing
This is a fluid method of working similar to monoprint. It entails covering a stiff sheet of paper evenly with a mixture of three parts rolling-up black to one part retransfer ink. This greasy black surface can now be:
(a) Scraped into, like a scraper board, so when transferred on a plate, white lines of drawing will appear against a black background.
(b) *Gently* turned over on to a prepared plate and drawn through, as with carbon paper, so the black ink will print where pressure has been applied.

Many variations of these two drawing methods are possible with this mix of ink and if the retransfer ink appears too stiff, the mix can be softened using ordinary mineral oil such as '3 in 1'.

PLATE PROCESSING

The standard procedure for processing a plate is as follows:
(a) Dust the drawn image with French chalk.
(b) Thinly gum the plate with fresh gum arabic.
(c) Leave for fifteen minutes.
(d) Using pure turpentine, remove pigment from the drawing grease rubbing gently with a rag. Reinforce the adsorbed grease layer with a thin coating of asphaltum.
(e) Take the plate to the sink and remove the surface gum and the unwanted dry asphaltum with water and a rag.
(f) Remove excess water with a sponge, revealing the image under a thin coat of asphaltum.
(g) Carefully roll up the damp plate with stiff non-drying black. Once the plate is evenly rolled up, dry and print.

PLATE PROOFING

It normally now takes three 'proofs' for an image to appear fully charged with ink, giving a wide tonal variety, on paper. Ink build up on the plate should be gradual. Generally speaking, a sparse application of all chemicals, gums, water and inks to a plate will achieve the best result.

Procedure for rolling up
(a) A thin stiffish layer of non-drying rolling up black is rolled on to the slab with a clean nap roller (a small quantity of Chalk Black or magnesia powder can be added to stiffen).
(b) Slightly dampen the plate and roll up with a gentle pressure in several directions (to eliminate roller marks). Then repeat.
(c) The image should now be fully visible in black, ready to print.

Procedure for proofing
(a) Place the rolled up plate on the bed of the press and cover with a sheet of proofing paper (newsprint is ideal for first proofs).
(b) Cover the proofing paper with at least five sheets of paper to act as backing. These cushion the pressure and keep the print clean.
(c) Lower the tympan over the bed and slide the press bed until the scraper bar is just over the edge of the bed.
(d) Adjust the pressure so that when the pressure lever is pulled down, the scraper is in firm contact with the tympan.
(e) Having checked that the tympan is greasy, wind the plate through the press under firm pressure.
(f) Check the print and continue until a fully charged print is taken.

Judging correct inking and proofing comes from experience and below is a guide to help the inexperienced printer.

1. Dusting the image with French chalk.

2. Gumming the plate with gum arabic.

3. Removing pigment with turpentine.

4. Reinforcing image with asphaltum.

5. Rinsing with water.

6. Rolling out non-drying ink.

7. Rolling plate with non-drying black.

8. Dampening plate.

9. Rolling ink.

10. Laying paper over print. 119,221

11. Moving the tympan.

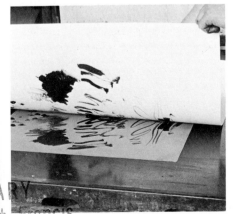
12. Revealing the print.

25

PRINTING & PROOFING PROBLEMS

Problem	Possible cause	Treatment
Image too filled in	Over-inking	Damp plate well, roll off excess ink by a quick rolling.
	Excess pressure	Reduce pressure.
	Excess asphaltum	Wash out with pure turps. Roll up, print.
	Excess extender	Clean slab and plate. Re-roll with a stiffer ink.
Image too light	Ink too stiff	Add extender or soft varnish to ink.
	Too little pressure	Increase pressure.
	Over etched	Resensitise. Redraw.
	Degreased image (water left on a washed out proof too long)	Resensitise. Redraw.
Streaks on image	Faulty scraper bar	Replace leather/wood.
	Damaged tympan	Replace or use more backing paper.
	Creased backing paper	Replace or straighten backing paper.

Plate etches

Once a good proof is pulled, it is possible to tell if the plate will need 'etching'. The sole purpose of etching is to clean the background of the plate of any unwanted matter. Two forms of etch can be used, water etch or gum etch.

(1) Water etches
('Victory etch' (tannic acid and water); Commercial plate etch)
The stronger of the two forms of etch, these must be well reduced with water before application. For protection, the image is dusted with resin and French chalk. A generous amount of etch is constantly agitated on the plate and left there no longer than three minutes. A pumice stick or powder can be used in conjunction with the etch at this stage to remove any stubborn marks. Finally, the water etch is completely washed off the plate with water and the plate is gummed up with a thin coat of gum etch. The gum etch further cleans and desensitises the non-printing areas so the plate is now ready to print.
   Note: if a plate has been properly prepared and processed and the roller is clean and the ink fresh, it should *not* be necessary to use water etches at all. They certainly can be useful in certain circumstances but they tend to be overused resulting, often, in fluctuations occuring during the printing.

(2) Gum etches
('Atzol' (gallic acid and gum); 'Agum Z'; 1 ml phosphoric acid to 50 ml gum)
Most gum etches are essentially gum arabic with the addition of a little acid (tannic/gallic/phosphoric). They can be used directly on an image without the necessity of resin and French chalk although on a very tenuous layer of grease, it is advisable to add up to 50 per cent gum arabic. The slight acidity

of these etches helps keep the background of the plate sharp without attacking the image.

Gum arabic is one of the most important chemicals used in lithography. It is derived from the acacia tree family and is still the most effective plate desensitiser despite useful commercial equivalents such as Agum 'O'.

The gum comes in crystals or powder form and is placed in a stockinette-type straining bag and left for at least a day in *cold* water. Once dissolved, the gum should be of a creamy consistency and any impurities will be left in the bag. A few drops of carbolic acid will help preserve the made up gum for about six days.

Wash drawing and processing

For this type of drawing, it is most important that the wash is applied *as directly as possible* to the fresh plate. Much alteration will produce results that although appearing to have great tonal variety are in actuality almost solid.

This method of processing varies in two ways from the standard procedure.

(a) A further 1/20 'prepping' is done at least twice after the drawing has been initially gummed up and before processing commences.

(b) Pure turpentine, by itself, or with a little proofing black, is used in the place of asphaltum.

The further dilute prepping clarifies the wash thus keeping it from a tendency to 'fill in' once printing proceeds. Pure turpentine, with its oily grease attracting properties will help maintain a fine tonal balance as asphaltum has a tendency to thicken a wash drawing. Ideally, also, fresh gum arabic is used for all gumming up and no water etches are used. As long as action is taken immediately, gum arabic will clear any scum should it occur on the image.

This procedure in processing is highly effective on a wide variety of drawn images and it is to be noted that the subtlety and directness of any 'drawing' has the least potential chemical interference.

DELETIONS & ADDITIONS

At the drawing stage

Before the plate has been processed and the grease fully established either abrasive or chemical means can be used to remove unwanted work. A plastic rubber, pumice powder or an Etcho stick with water are used to carefully rub away unwanted work or alternatively MEK or benzine are applied to dissolve the unwanted area. The plate is then cleaned with a 1/20 dilution of Prepasol before gumming up.

At the printing stage

The plate should be rolled up in proofing black, which has a strong resistance to acids and gummed up. As abrasive methods will tend to smear ink, the chemical method (as above) is best used. Due to the grease being well established, a neat solution of 'Erasol' (caustic potash) should also be applied to the area. A glass fibre brush is used to apply this caustic and it should be left on the plate for four or five minutes. The plate is then washed clean and prepped and gummed as above.

Redrawing after deleting

The following strengths of counter-etch are necessary.

(1) For zinc and aluminium: Prepasol (nitric acid/potash alum) 1:10 parts water; phosphoric acid and water 1:100 parts water.

(2) Aluminium only: oxalic acid and water 1:20 parts water.

It is advisable to apply at least two applications of counter-etch to the plate.

Evergreen, Hampton Court.
Hand-drawn lithograph in 8 colours 20″ × 14″
John Tetley.

LITHOGRAPHY

PHOTO LITHOGRAPHY

The coating of grained zinc and aluminium plates with egg albumen or ammonium bichromate to make a photo sensitive surface has been largely superseded by the use of mechanically coated anodised aluminium plates. These more predictable commercially used plates are widely available with complete simplified processing systems. Most artists will use a commercial plate maker to make up the images on a plate from the artwork unless able to use the facilities of a workshop or art school. Two types of artwork can be used on a photo-plate, photo images and drawn images.

Photo images
(a) A continuous tone photograph has first to be reprinted via a 'dot' screen to produce areas of broken tone on transparent film. This black and white breakdown of a photograph is essential for manual printing in lithography.
(b) The film is brought into contact with the photosensitive emulsion on the plate by use of a vacuum frame.
(c) The image is transferred to the plate under controlled exposure from an ultra violet light source (carbon arc/halogen quartz).

The ultra violet light hardens the photosensitive emulsion on the plate, where it has been exposed, enabling the soft emulsion under the image to be removed and replaced by an ink attracting surface during the processing.

Drawn images
This is a commonly used method in many art schools and workshops. By this method a drawing is done on a thin grained semi-transparent plastic sheet ('Kodatrace', 'Draft-film' etc.) using light opaque materials (litho chalk, photo opaque, gouache). The drawing is then transferred to the plate as above. Exposure times are less for most drawn images than for photo images so as to 'burn out' as little drawing as possible.

Although excellent for any high contrast images, tonally varied drawings done by this method are never as successful as their counterparts drawn on ordinary plate. This is due to the crude nature of rolling up anodised plate by hand and to the high contrast type developers which are only now being superseded by a more tonal type. Despite the success of these new developers, in bringing up remarkably detailed results on the plate, it is necessary to print from a self-inking/damping offset machine to pull up all these qualities on paper. The softness of ink necessary is simply too fluid for hand rolling.

COLOUR LITHOGRAPHY

Before the non-drying black is washed out of the plate, it is important to roll out the desired colour on the slab with a composition/glazed leather roller. Most inks, being made for machine printing are too soft and so must be stiffened with magnesia powder or stiff litho varnish to avoid any scumming. The following procedure should then be used to ensure that all the black is washed out of the plate.

Wet washout
(a) Take the plate to the sink and cover it with water.
(b) Turps should be applied and gently rubbed over the image so removing all the black ink from the damp plate.
(c) Remove the ink, sponge the excess water down to an even layer.
(d) A thin coat of asphaltum or pure turps should then be applied across the plate and on to the adsorbed grease.
(e) Sponge the plate again with water, it is now ready to roll up in colour.

If a light, transparent colour is to be used, a clear washout solution or pure turpentine with a little of the colour is used for asphaltum can discolour light ink. At the end of each day the plate must be rolled up in non drying black and gummed up. If colour is left on a plate overnight, it is possible to remove using a few drops of carbolic acid and turpentine.

Inks
Most lithographic inks are transparent. They can be made further transparent by the addition of reducing medium or opaque by the addition of white. If the ink is too stiff (adhering weakly and unevenly to the plate) a small amount of wax ('Platene') or thin varnish can be added.

Colour printing
A colour will dry in approximately eight hours. If further printing is essential sooner, it is better to dust the fresh prints with anti set-off powder – to protect further plates from adhering to the wet print – than to use extra driers in the ink.

Although important to plan the stages of a colour print as far as possible, it is essential to be open to possible changes in the order of printing both plates and colours. Often, as with the use of transparent colour over-printing, it is difficult to predict the tone and sometimes the colour until the overprinting is done.

While each plate is normally rolled up in one colour, provided the grease is spaced apart on the plate, it is possible to roll up different colours on the one plate. This requires the use of small rollers (brayers). For certain effects, it is also possible to make a rainbow of different colours on the inking slab and by steady careful rolling to transfer this effect to the plate.

REGISTRATION METHODS

This is most important for colour lithography where each colour is normally drawn up on a separate plate. Several methods can be used to align the paper to the plates, the most common being the registration cross method.

Registration crosses
By this method two finely drawn crosses are drawn on the plate at the drawing stage, one either side of the image and at least 4 cm (1·58 in) away from the work. When the first colour has been printed, the paper is cut through on each print along the cross lines and a triangular segment is cut from each cross. The paper can now be accurately laid to successive plates by visual alignment through the back to the corresponding cross on the plate.

Pin hole registration
This method is used to avoid any unsightly cutting on good quality paper. It is initially similar to the above method though with dots of ink in place of the crosses. Two needles are passed through each registration 'dot' on the print and the paper is then pulled taut and carefully laid on the plate using the needles as guides to the 'dots'. It is helpful to lightly punch the dots on further plates to accept the needles. Only a minute hole will be visible by this method and dots of ink, once dry, can easily be removed from the paper using a little flour paper or a plastic rubber.

Tracing
This involves using one key tracing from the original drawing. The tracing, which is set down in turn on each of the separate plates, must have registration marks on. Each plate is covered by a sheet of chalk paper (carbon paper if a printing line is required) and the line tracing is secured on top to prevent any movement. The drawing is now set down by firm retracing with a hard pencil or ball point pen, through the two layers. It is to be remembered that

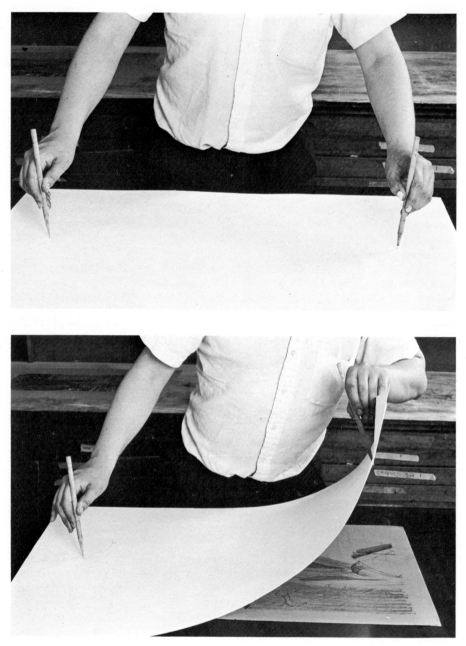

Registering the plate using the pinhole method.

the tracing must be reversed on to the plate, when a direct press is used, to print the correct way round.

Offset registration

This is an effective method of registration for images printed by the offset method as the paper is left completely unmarked. A piece of acetate, the size of the paper bed, is clamped in the paper grippers along one side and pulled taut to be hinge taped to the bed along the opposite side. The plate is rolled up in the colour and printed via the offset blanket on to the acetate. Printing paper can now be slipped under the acetate, aligned with the image, and clamped in the grippers while the acetate is hinged back under the offset blanket to await the next print. The image is now printed directly on to the paper.

Set-off powder

This method is excellent for offsetting a complex image accurately to further plates.

Right: A selection of papers showing differing texture and weave.

(a) The initial plate – with registration crosses – is printed on a smooth unabsorbent paper in non-drying black. One light proof is done per colour.
(b) While the proofs are still wet, a dessertspoonful of methyl violet dye is rocked across the printed image until it has adhered to all the wet ink.
(c) Surplus powder is poured on to the next proof and by flicking the back of each proof and running dry fine sand across the surface, all excess powder is removed.
(d) A fresh plate is damped with a 75 per cent water to 25 per cent methylated spirits mix and fanned almost dry.
(e) A dusted proof is now placed face down on the plate and passed through the press once so that a light powder image, a replica of the initial plate, is transferred.

Methyl violet, being a strong dye, should be kept well away from any work surfaces or clean paper. The powder should not be used if it has become damp as it takes on a lumpy quality which will affect any drawing if it is transferred to the plate.

PAPERS

Papers used in lithography can be divided into three categories, machine-made, mould-made and handmade. Although most artists will initially use the cheaper and often very adequate machine-made papers at the proofing stage, the majority will prefer to produce final lithographs on good quality paper.

Machine-made
Three useful types of machine-made paper are listed below.
(1) Newsprint, an unsized wood paper. This is the cheapest and one of the most useful papers used in lithography. Although it discolours quickly, it is ideal for initial proofing or as a backing or interleaving paper.
(2) Cartridge paper is again a much used paper which is available with a variety of surfaces. A soft surface should be used in lithography as much cartridge paper is heavily sized to withstand drawing and is not very absorbent. The best quality can be used for editions.
(3) Machine glazed (MG) paper is another useful paper. This has a smooth side, ideal for offsets and a rougher, more absorbent side, for direct printing.

Some wood free, machine-made paper is made but most, being made of wood pulp, will tend to yellow in time.

Mould-made
This is the most widely used paper for editions and it is essentially a rag (cotton) paper. It is rare to find *completely* unsized or 'waterleaf' mould-made or handmade paper now, most is either 'soft' sized or 'hard' sized and available in three surfaces: HP (hot pressed), NOT (not hot pressed) and rough. For lithography, only the HP paper should be used, both NOT and rough are too uneven to pick up accurately from a grained surface. Mould-made paper is distinguished from machine-made by a watermark in the paper and often by a deckle edge along two sides or more. The choice of sizing in the paper depends on the nature of the drawing – hard sized paper being excellent for strong chalk work, soft sized for washes.

Handmade
This paper is now becoming increasingly rare and consequently expensive. Handmade papers have an irregular deckled edge and tend to vary slightly in thickness. For this reason, editions are mostly printed on the more consistent mould-made paper. The little true waterleaf paper that is still made, tends to be handmade and this is glazed between sheets of zinc and not sized. This paper needs most careful handling as it will easily absorb dirty marks and cockle if allowed to get damp.

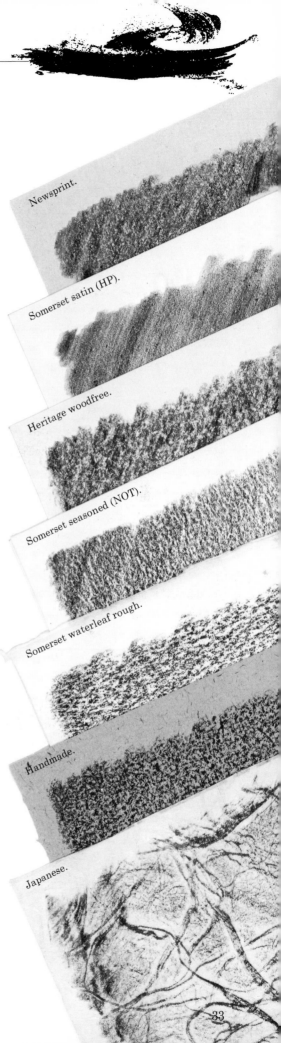

Newsprint.

Somerset satin (HP).

Heritage woodfree.

Somerset seasoned (NOT).

Somerset waterleaf rough.

Handmade.

Japanese.

ETCHING AND ENGRAVING

ETCHING AND ENGRAVING

By scratching, incising or eroding the surface of a flat sheet of metal it is possible to obtain indentations. This plate can then be inked to allow these indentations to hold ink and the rest of the plate to be wiped clean. A print can then be taken on paper using a copperplate press. Printing from below the surface of the metal in this manner is known as Intaglio Printing.

The copperplate print or etching as it is more commonly known is instantly recognisable by one characteristic. On the paper is an indentation, which is the mark of the plate pressed into the paper as the plate and paper together move through the rollers of the press. The enormous pressure involved forces the damp, therefore softened, paper to extract the ink from the lines and other marks etched into the surface on the plate. This indentation has become its trademark.

STUDIO EQUIPMENT

When it comes to etching a variety of equipment is needed, but above all else the first consideration should be the press. Presses and the blankets used with them are expensive items and are therefore not available to everyone immediately. People today use the facilities belonging to a variety of establishments, some educational or professional. Print workshops and co-operatives offer the use of their equipment for a reasonable fee. Print co-operatives have sprung up over the last few years, thanks to Arts Council, local council and private grants and are very welcome to the printmaker.

If, however, you do decide to buy a press of your own, the choice is between new or old. New presses are readily available, but are, of course, the most expensive. Of the many fine presses on the market a few that spring readily to mind are Chris Holliday's good looking Modbury Press, Harry Rochat's fine range of presses, and the Hunter Penrose collection. On the other hand, a second-hand press does become available now and again, but a good one will still fetch a high price.

What to look for when buying a press? Most importantly, it must take a good print. This may seem obvious, so why not take a print; it will tell you a great deal about the press; whether the rollers are worn and concave, whether the bed is still flat and if the gears actually mesh. However, if in doubt it would be wise to have a professional look over it with you. This will be your biggest expenditure and it is worth taking time and advice over your decision.

Presses are heavy and will need firm, level ground to sit on. If it is to be used on a suspended wooden floor, then spreading the weight by some means of support would be advisable to make it safe. It would be disastrous one morning to find your beloved press was no longer on the top floor, but had decided of its own accord to spend some time in the basement!

Press blankets are made from pure wool and should be woven. They come in various thicknesses and are usually cut to size. As to the number of blankets used this does vary. When I print I usually use two facings (thin blankets) with one swanskin (thick blanket). I have seen this varied from three facings and one swanskin, to two facings and two swanskins. When printing, blankets will pick up size from the damp paper and must be washed regularly to ensure that they do not become stiff. Ideally they should be soaked in some softener and handwashed, then laid flat to dry. In a hurry, I have had them drycleaned, but I usually machine-wash them in warm water with soapflakes and extra water softener and then tumble-dry them.

More basic materials are considerably less expensive than the press and it is essential to establish all these in the studio, starting with the 'plate'. The best known metal for etching is copper, followed by zinc and then steel. These three metals, together with aluminium and perspex make it possible to produce any type of intaglio print.

Suppliers of plate are numerous and it is advisable to shop around for the best prices available; of course, the more you buy the cheaper it is. It may,

The Modbury Etching Press – 1981.

The Hunter Penrose Etching press.

therefore, be advantageous for several people to get together to buy in large quantities, not just the metal but many of the other materials as well. Large sheets of metal can be cut by the supplier at an extra cost, but make enquiries at your nearest print studio or art school, they may be able to offer advice. The gauge used for intaglio printing varies from 16 gauge (1.6 mm) to 20 gauge (0.8 mm), the most popular being 18 gauge (1.2 mm). Zinc is usually sold in 40 × 20 inch sheets (1020 × 510 mm). Sheet mild steel comes in any size and is usually unpolished, but if you want it polished there are metal merchants who will do this.

For biting copper there are two popular acids, one is Dutch Mordant and

The Fish vase.
Coloured aquatint 20″ × 25″
Frank Tinsley.

Stoneware pot.
Coloured etching 30″ × 21″
Frank Tinsley.

the other is Iron Pechloride, sometimes called Ferric Chloride (not strictly an acid, but a salt which rots the metal). Dutch Mordant is recommended because the biting action of the acid gives off no bubbles and this minimises any underbiting of the wax ground. It bites very slowly and a careful eye must be kept on delicate areas for any foul biting (the acid biting in unwanted areas) which is normally detectable when using other acids by the bubbles that would appear. The recipe most commonly used for mixing Dutch Mordant is ten parts saturated potassium chlorate crystals to one part hydrochloric acid, the acid will turn green after use.

Ferric Chloride/Iron Pechloride is a brown opaque liquid, which makes it impossible to see the plate when it is immersed. Another disadvantage is that, after a short time, a deposit forms in the line stopping the bite. The line must be cleaned out by rinsing under water before continuing. In ferric acid it is usual to lay the plate face down to allow the deposit to fall out of its own accord. To do this you should build a platform from matchsticks and tape, or plasticine to raise the plate off the bottom of the tray allowing the acid easy access. When laying the plate in the acid face down, make sure there are no air bubbles trapped underneath as these would stop the acid from biting and give a patchy etch.

Personally, I much prefer to place the plate face upward, and using a 5 or 8 cm (2 or 3 in) wide housebrush, gently stroke the plate. This stroking action removes the deposit allowing the salt to attack the plate and speeds up an otherwise lengthy biting process. There is no gas given off with Iron Pechloride in the etching process, and for that reason is very useful in confined areas and avoids the need for a sophisticated extraction system.

Nitric acid can be used on copper plates for fairly coarse biting only, as the action is quite violent. I would, therefore, not recommend it for fine work of any kind as the bite can sometimes be uncontrollable. However, when using zinc plates, nitric acid is best.

Acid strengths

The recommended strength for Iron Pechloride for copper is 45° Beaume and I use it straight from the container. Like most acids it is best not left out overnight as it evaporates changing its strength and consistency.

The best solution when using zinc in nitric acid is between seven to nine parts water, to one part acid. This is ideal for most etching work. The acid is extremely corrosive in its undiluted form and must never be used this way as the fumes are extremely obnoxious and toxic. The golden rule when mixing the solution is ALWAYS ADD ACID TO WATER, NEVER WATER TO ACID. Never pour diluted acid into an undiluted bottle, always keep them separate and well marked showing strength and acid. Use rubber gloves when mixing acids and keep the extractor or ventilator on. If you spill acid on your body or clothes, then copious amounts of water will dilute it. If in doubt, seek medical attention. It is good to get into the habit of wearing a good strong plastic apron when mixing acids.

For biting sheet mild steel nitric is best used at the same strength as for zinc, but you must remember to use separate baths for zinc and steel – nitric used on zinc remains clear, and on steel turns brown. When zinc is exposed to nitric acid the resultant exchange is a gas which can be seen as bubbles. This is hydrogen gas. These bubbles must be continuously wiped from the line using a feather or soft fibreglass brush, otherwise you will find that the line when printed will take on the appearance of a beaded necklace. This is because the bubble itself is acid resistant and the acid is forced to bite around it, giving an uneven line.

The question of how long should a plate be left in the acid is a very difficult one to answer. I have found that a test plate, usually an offcut or scrap of the metal being used, with bites varying between thirty seconds to thirty minutes will give a good indication of what to expect. However, it is only an indication, and no definitive times should be assumed, as there are many factors which control the length of time in the acid. The strength of the acid

may change from day to day, from either evaporation leaving a more potent brew, or continuous use which weakens it. Temperature may affect its strength, the warmer the room the quicker the acid will bite, and conversely, the lower the temperature the slower it will bite. One person I knew would add a little warm water to the acid bath in the winter just to 'spice it up'.

Keeping factors as constant as possible will help when timing the bite of a plate, although this will be more difficult in a crowded studio or where the acid is in an outbuilding where changes in temperature occur daily. Several plates in an acid will also cause problems with timing, as the action of the bite makes the acid warmer, therefore speeding up the etching process. Once the acid is overworked or depleted it is best to mix up a fresh batch but be careful as a freshly mixed acid tends to be 'sharp'. It is best to keep a little of the old acid to add to the new mix to take the edge off it.

The most common acid bath used is made from plastic which is light, useful when it comes to emptying out old acid. Stainless steel or ceramic baths are also available.

Inks

Intaglio inks can be bought ready-made in a variety of colours in quantities ranging from 250 g to 1 kg (approx. 9 oz to 2·2 lb). Charbonnel of France offer a good range of intaglio inks of high quality.

However, I prefer to mix my own inks from the powdered pigments which can be bought in small quantities from printmaking suppliers, it is cheaper to do this and I can alter the consistency more easily. Mixing inks is not difficult, and all that is needed is the pigment, copperplate oil, a broad spatula and a muller for grinding the ink and the oil together, plus a sheet of thick glass. Black will become the basic stock in trade ink and, therefore, I will discuss mixing this colour first. A well-proven mixture of one third Heavy French and two thirds Frankfurt Black will give an ink that will be useful for most printing and proofing. Most printmakers do, of course, have their own special mix that suits them, in the course of time no doubt you will find your own favourite.

Adding copperplate oil.

(1) Mixing the black ink

Method – once you have mixed the dry pigments together add a little copperplate oil. This comes in four consistencies, thick, medium, thin and raw. I always add thick first and then, if necessary, a little thin oil to make it easier to use. Add a little oil at a time until all the pigment is taken up by the oil, working it well with the spatula. Once you have got a thickish sticky consistency it is ready for mulling. Glass mullers are available, but I have seen bits of rounded lithography stone put to great effect here. The idea is to mull a little at a time to produce a smooth shiny ink that does not fall easily from the palette knife. This can then be used right away or stored in an airtight container. I sometimes put a little water on top to stop the air from getting at the ink and forming a skin. When you want to use the ink and it is difficult to spread on the plate, then a little thin oil mixed in will help. You will find the ink will 'move' a little more readily on a warm day and be a bit 'tacky' on a cold day.

Mixing the pigments.

(2) Mixing the colours

The ready prepared inks for colour printing are, of course, time and labour saving, but if you are mixing them from powdered pigments then the same procedure applies as for mixing the black. Mulling is not always necessary with some of the finer colour pigments as they mix up very easily giving a smooth stiff paste.

Copper and especially zinc, unlike steel, have a tendency to oxidise with certain pigments and change the colour. This is seen particularly with colours such as white becoming grey and yellow becoming green. The earth colours, however, such as browns and ochres are not affected greatly and will print in a stable manner. Making sure the plate is clean before printing is helpful and lighter fluid can be very useful here. Steel facing the copper

Ink mulling.

ETCHING AND ENGRAVING

Above: *Blue table*.
Coloured etching 23½″ × 33½″
Tim Mara.

Right: *Lily*.
Coloured aquatint 30″ × 21″
Frank Tinsley.

will prevent this oxidation process. So the proof on copper may well be different from the print taken after steel facing.

Reducing medium or tinteen is added when you wish to make a colour transparent. However, if a lot is added it can make wiping difficult in lightly bitten areas, it becomes sticky and hard to move.

If you are editioning, make up enough ink for all your edition. There is nothing more frustrating than running out of a colour halfway through and trying to mix up the same colour again. When mixing colours for an edition, it would be wise to make notes of the proportions used and keep colour dabs for matching.

Oil colours can sometimes be used, but their thin consistency means they are easily wiped out of the etched area.

ETCHING

Preparing the plate

For most line drawings a wax resist is used known as a hard ground. It is made from a mixture of beeswax, resin and bitumen. This ground is necessary for the protection of the plate in the acid and allows the acid to etch only where the metal has been exposed by drawing.

In preparing the plate for etching the edges must initially be filed to take away the sharpness left by the guillotine. These sharp edges will cut you, the paper and the blankets if left. Final bevelling and polishing can be done later when the plate is ready for editioning.

Before applying the hard ground the plate needs to be degreased to make sure the ground adheres properly and will not lift off in the acid causing unwanted biting known euphemistically as foul-biting. A paste is made from whiting, ammonia and water which is spread and rubbed into the plate with a piece of cottonwool. After twenty or thirty seconds, depending on the size of the plate, rinse the plate with clean water. If it is degreased properly the water will stay evenly over the whole surface. The plate is then put on a hot-plate and is wiped with a clean piece of cottonwool until it dries. If streaks appear this probably means that the plate has not been rinsed thoroughly.

Grounds

The hard ground which comes in blocks is spread over the heated plate and evened out with a leather roller. The hotplate should be hot enough to melt the wax freely but burning or smouldering should be avoided. My own hotplate is set at 70°C. The quicker you roll the thinner the coating. If the ground becomes too hot and liquid, the roller will slide, and the plate should be moved to the jigger and allowed to become cool. The roller should then be slowly applied to re-establish the ground. The finished ground should be deep in colour and smooth. There is also a proprietary liquid ground that is brushed on to the plate with a soft brush. Left to dry at an angle most of the brush marks will eventually disappear.

Smoking a plate is done for the purpose of making the hard ground even darker so the colour of the plate will show in contrast through the ground when drawing. To smoke a plate, hold the plate aloft in a hand vice and allow the soot from the lighted tapers to mix with the ground and form a shiny enamel-like finish. After smoking the plate should the surface appear sooty, move it back on to the hot plate and re-heat it. The reason for a ground appearing sooty is that the plate was allowed to cool too much before smoking. To transfer a pencil drawing, place it face down on the prepared plate. Cover with a piece of blotting paper. Then wind through the press; the pencil line will be seen on the darkened ground.

Drawing into the ground is done to expose the plate underneath and allow the acid to bite. The depth of the bite and, therefore, the strength of the printed line, depends on how long it is left in the acid. Care should be taken

1. Degreasing plate.

2. Applying hard ground.

3. Rolling out hard ground.

4. Smoking plate.

5. Drawing on hard ground.

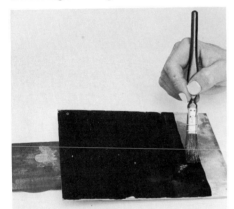

6. Stopping out back of plate.

7. Plate in acid.

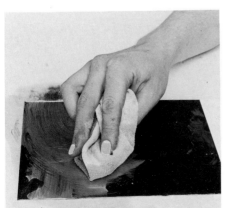

8. Cleaning off hardground and stopout varnish.

when drawing not to scratch the plate, as these scratches could catch the ink and subsequently print. If you are dissatisfied with your drawing, regrounding is an easy solution, but only if you are sure there are no scratches from the first attempt which may show up when printing.

Once the drawing is complete the reverse side of the plate must be stopped out with varnish. Some metals come with an acid resistant coating already applied, avoiding the need for varnishing. Unless the back is varnished the plate in the acid provokes the bubbling activity unnecessarily and results in a 'hotting up' of the acid. Timing an etch under these conditions becomes difficult and sometimes impossible. The intensive bubbling action can even undermine and tear off the ground causing extensive foul-biting. Variations in the depth of the line can be obtained by several immersions in the acid. By using the stop-out varnish, different parts of the plate can be painted out and after drying re-immersed to allow the rest of the exposed drawing to continue etching. The complete drawing does not have to be etched all at once. Thus the process allows you to etch part of the drawing, proof it, then if necessary to reground, to continue drawing and further etching until the plate is completed. When regrounding a plate it is unnecessary to smoke it as this will conceal the already etched areas.

Soft ground is made from the same ingredients as the hard ground but with an added measure of tallow. This allows the ground when cold to remain soft and malleable unlike the enamel finish of the hard ground. Since it remains soft it will take an impression of anything it is likely to come into contact with. As you will find to your cost if you handle the plate without care – you will have perfect impressions of your thumb prints! It goes without saying that transporting a soft ground plate is very difficult, if not impossible.

Preparing the plate for soft ground does not necessitate thorough degreasing, however it will do no harm to be on the safe side. Applying soft ground is the same as for hard ground, but because of the tallow, if heated too much the roller will skid along the surface of the plate leaving an unsatisfactory finish. If this happens allow the plate to cool down a little, then continue rolling slowly to re-establish the ground. Once cooled it is ready to use. You do not need to smoke a soft ground. Use a different roller for each ground and keep them clearly marked.

The most obvious reason for using soft ground is to impress textures into its surface. These can range from feathers and crumpled silver paper to coarse weave materials and dried flowers. After laying the chosen material or texture cover the whole thing with stencil or greaseproof paper. This stops any of the ground adhering to the blankets. This is to stop the soft ground being picked up on the blankets because now the plate is rolled through the press to impress the texture into the ground. Normal printing pressure is usually too much for soft ground impressions, so removing one of the blankets will be necessary before rolling the plate slowly through. Once you have removed the textures you will see their impressions in the ground. Using the stop-out varnish again you can define which particular parts of the impression you want to etch. It is also good policy to block out any parts of the plate where the greaseproof paper may have accidentally impressed itself into the ground.

When biting the plate and the tell-tale bubbles appear, do not wipe these away as you may easily scratch the soft ground and allow the acid to foul-bite. Getting rid of these bubbles usually means gently removing the plate from the acid, and allowing them to disappear before returning the plate for continued biting.

Another use for soft ground is to obtain a line similar, when printed, to a pencil or crayon drawing (unlike the hard ground needled line which looks similar to a pen drawing). To experiment with this method cover the prepared soft ground plate with tracing paper and being careful not to rest on it draw with a pencil or crayon using a fraction more pressure than when drawing on paper. This pressure will depend to some extent on the greasiness of the soft ground and the coarseness of paper to be used. To avoid leaning on

Just some of the materials that can be used in softground to obtain a variety of textures.

ETCHING AND ENGRAVING

the plate while drawing an ideal contraption for resting your arm on is a piece of wood supported either end by blocks giving sufficient height to clear the plate and paper. It is also wise to secure the tracing paper to the table or desk with tape. This allows you to check the impression of the drawing and alter it accordingly whilst ensuring that the paper goes back exactly in the same place.

It is possible to use both hard and soft ground techniques on the same plate but never at the same time. Also, remember to put the blanket back on the press after you have finished.

When drawing into grounds a wide variety of tools can be used and I suggest experimenting with needles, nails, wire wool, sandpaper, dentists' tools, turps, rats and snails and puppydogs' tails!

AQUATINTING

Hard and soft grounds are the methods by which linear or textured marks are obtained. A tone, however, is achieved by the use of aquatint. The main ingredient for aquatint is resin powder, its usefulness being that once heated it becomes acid resistant. Degrease the plate as for a hard ground and allow to dry. Application of the resin is done either by the box method or the bag method. The aquatint box is a wooden construction containing resin powder and by any of several means, in most cases a paddle, the resin is swept or blown from the well into the top of the box. The plate is then placed inside and the resin allowed to settle. The coarse particles fall first followed by the finer dust, and depending upon your own requirements, inserting and extracting the plate will become a matter for you to decide. I usually allow ten seconds for the larger particles to fall and then insert the plate leaving it for five minutes. I always lay the plate on a board to facilitate handling it in and out of the box. There are boxes which use bellows for churning up the resin or small home-made boxes where it is sufficient to turn them upside down a few times before putting in the plate.

The bag method allows greater control over the size of the resin powder used and distribution. For this I have several jars containing various grades

Handshaking the resin for a coarse aquatint.

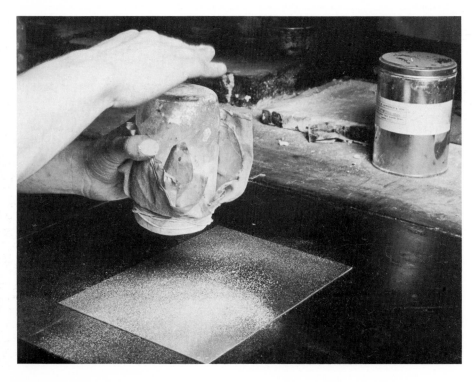

Right: *Easel.*
Etching with embossing 20″ × 30″
David Beevers.

of resin powder from fine to coarse, the tops are covered with tarleton, a coarse muslin, and secured with an elastic band. A jar is held over the plate away from any draft and lightly tapped or shaken allowing the resin to fall. If large grains are needed it is easy enough to sprinkle some from your fingers. The resin coating should cover about 50 per cent of the area to be etched.

The plate must then be heated, and this is best done with a gas poker on a low flame. The resin when 'cooked' becomes transparent and the poker should then be moved under the next area until the whole plate is finished. It is then left to cool. Having too high a flame may cause overcooking and grains of resin will float together instead of remaining separate. This heating adheres the resin particles to the plate and the acid will be forced to bite in between the particles producing a roughened surface, which when inked will print as a tone. The strength of this tone depends on how long the plate is etched.

To define the area of tone varnish can be used. This can be applied as with 'line etching' at several stages during the etch offering a wide range of tone. A few seconds in the acid will often roughen up the plate enough to print a slight tone.

One of the dangers of aquatinting is the occurrence of what is known as over-biting. This usually happens when trying for maximum roughness in order for it to print black.

Acid bites sideways as well as down and will undercut the particles of resin if the plate is left in the acid too long. If not checked the resin will lift off leaving a slightly uneven surface holding possibly enough ink to print a patchy grey. This point of maximum bite will vary depending on several factors. The amount of resin and strength of the acid are the two most obvious. A test plate is useful but it should be remembered that when dusting with a bag it is difficult to get the same covering on both. In using an aquatint box, however, both the test plate and the plate you are working on should be put in the box together to be sure that an equal amount of resin lands on both. And remember, a large exposed area of metal will bite quicker than a small one so a test plate 5 cm (2 in) square may not help you if the area intended for biting is 30 cm (12 in) square.

There are other resists besides varnish which can be used with equal effectiveness. Wax crayons will prevent the acid from biting giving a pleasant soft white line if used with an aquatint. This is best applied to a warm plate allowing the wax to run freely. Lithography crayons are excellent for this. Aerosol spray paints like those used for spraying cars are useful as they offer the chance of gradations in tone and give especially pleasant soft edges when sprayed over stencils.

Tones can be obtained using these sprays, as the fine spray affords approximately the same protection as the resin dust allowing the acid to bite in between the paint droplets, useful if there is no resin available. Sprays should be used in a well-ventilated room as the fumes can be very irritating.

Straight lines in tonal work can be obtained using a sticky backed plastic, such as Transpaseal or Fablon. Transpaseal is better because its transparency allows the drawing underneath to be seen. It can be cut with a knife or pair of scissors and the sticky back peeled off; it is then stuck down on to the plate, making sure the edges are secure. Patterns or designs can then be cut out using a craft knife. It has the advantage of resisting a lot of heat so resin can be added after it has been stuck down. A method of aquatinting I use frequently is to lay stencils on the plate before depositing the resin. The stencils are removed before heating.

The plate is then etched to the desired tone, the resin is cleaned off with meths and the plate polished. The areas which have no resin will have been 'open bitten', i.e. they will have no rough texture to hold the ink and will print white. This produces an image with a 'soft' edge difficult to obtain in any other way.

If you draw into the resin powder on the plate before fusing the etch it produces is defined as a white line in a dark tone.

Sugar aquatint

So far, all the drawing has had to be done in reverse, i.e. painting out around the area to be etched. A difficult procedure for the beginner to master initially. Sugar aquatint is used when it is wished to work in a positive way, i.e. painting the area actually to be etched with a sugar solution. Recipes do vary but the one I use is a small quantity of saturated sugar solution (sugar dissolved in water), with liquid gum (for example Gloy), a squirt of washing up liquid (which breaks down the surface tension) and black ink or poster paint for colouring. I also add a little whiting to help it dry quicker. When this has settled the consistency should be that of single cream. It can be applied with a brush or a pen. If the area to be etched is wanted as a tone, prepare the plate as normal for aquatinting, i.e. degrease the plate and fuse on a resin ground. When it has cooled paint on the sugar solution where you want the tone and allow to dry. I generally leave it overnight. The next step is to cover the plate with an acid resistant ground. I know of three ways that are successful and it is a matter of personal choice which you use. The first is to apply a thin coat of liquid hard ground to the whole plate and let it dry. The second is to paint on stop out varnish thinned out with meths, and thirdly to heat up the plate and roll on a hard ground. The plate is then laid in warm water where after a time the sugar solution will expand and begin lifting off the plate, taking with it the acid resist and exposing the resin covered plate underneath. This can now be etched to the required tone. If the sugar is hesitant in lifting off then gently stroke with a soft-haired brush.

It is worth remembering that when you are painting the sugar solution on to the plate and you find that your drawing is not satisfactory, you may wash the solution away with clean water. The resin coating underneath will not be affected.

Drypointing

The most direct way to make a print is to scratch on to a copperplate with a heavy steel needle or diamond point. As the needle is drawn through the plate, copper is pushed up on to the surface. This is known as the 'burr'.

The plate is then inked to allow the ink to collect around these scratches and the rest of the plate is wiped clean. There is no acid or ground involved. It is as dramatic as it is simple! The line is best described as 'furry' similar to a line drawing in charcoal. The line is rich and forceful and cannot be

Dry pointing with partially inked plate.

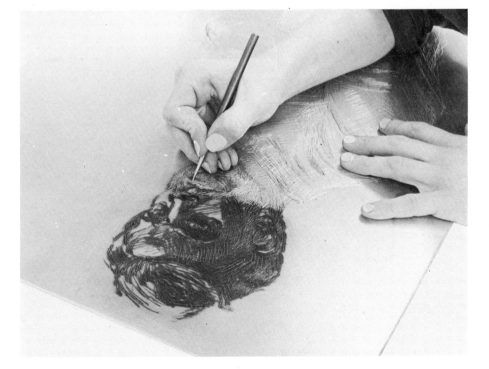

ETCHING AND ENGRAVING

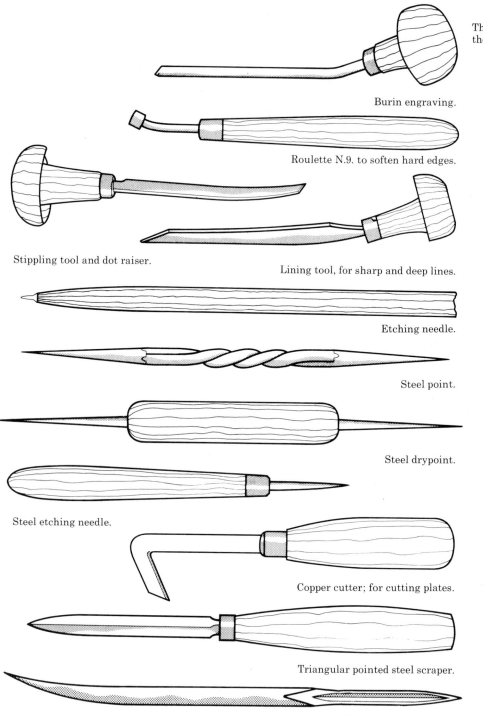

The selection of tools available can provide the etcher with a wide range of marks.

Burin engraving.

Roulette N.9. to soften hard edges.

Stippling tool and dot raiser.

Lining tool, for sharp and deep lines.

Etching needle.

Steel point.

Steel drypoint.

Steel etching needle.

Copper cutter; for cutting plates.

Triangular pointed steel scraper.

Steelscraper burnisher.

mistaken for any of the other intaglio processes. Drypointing is unique in copperplate printing as it is not truly intaglio, as most of the ink that is printed is caught in the burr raised by the needle and, therefore, sits on the surface of the plate.

This unmistakable quality, however, soon disappears after limited printing as the burr is extremely delicate and will wear quickly, leaving a lighter and thinner looking print. Proofing a drypoint is done only when necessary, taking care not to be heavy handed in inking and wiping. This heavy-handedness is, I am sure, the reason for many prematurely bald plates, and not altogether the fault of the press.

If a large edition is to be taken from a drypoint it is necessary to have it

steel-faced. This is when a very thin coat of steel is electrolytically deposited on to the copper plate, thin enough not to interfere with the drawing but thick enough to form a shield. This steel-facing allows a larger number of prints to be taken, far more than would be possible from the bare copper. You would not normally get more than ten to twelve prints from an unprotected copperplate, but after steel-facing you could expect to get in the region of thirty to thirty-five. The steel will wear and it is possible to have the plate re-steel-faced so lengthening the life of the plate. There is, when printing, a tendency to overwipe drypoints, not realising that the ink will, in a correctly wiped plate, be sitting on the surface of the plate and the line will have a different appearance to an etched line. The intention is to catch the ink in the burr, not wipe it clean.

Drypoints can also be drawn on steel, a much stronger metal than copper, requiring a diamond point or carbide tip. It is obvious that many more prints will be possible from a steel plate. Other substitutes can be found in aluminium or perspex. These materials are softer and easier to draw into than steel, but the burr will wear quickly and cannot be strengthened except by redrawing. The perspex offers considerable resistance to the steel needle and may only be useful for drypoints where a more fluid line is not needed. When printing from perspex plates it is advisable to dilute the ink with thin oil, making inking and wiping easier and heat cannot be used with any great effect. Less pressure is needed to print any drypoint, so remember to adjust the press.

Printing

There are two practical elements in etching, the first is making the plate which I have discussed above, the second is printing it. If you are extremely fortunate you could have someone do it for you: however, most of us have to do it ourselves. Good professional printers are worth their weight in gold (or copper if you prefer), and time spent watching someone print will prove invaluable from the point of view of economy and approach to a problem.

Organisation is the key to successful printing and preparation is the keyword.

The pressure must be set to give an all round even indentation in the paper and fine adjustments can be made after the first print has been taken. Mark out the bed for correct registration with either waterproof markers or straw hat varnish.

The paper should preferably be damped the day before. I usually soak the paper for about twenty to thirty minutes, drain and lightly sponge each sheet and lay them under cover, i.e. a plastic or rubber sheeting and a board to give some weight. If you anticipate leaving damp paper for more than two or three days, it is advisable to add a few drops of mould retarder, such as formaldehyde, to the water.

By the next day it should need only a light blotting, or brush over with a soft clean shoe brush kept especially for the purpose. This will also pick up the nap of the paper. Remember the paper is damped to make it soft, not to make it wet; therefore any excess water on the surface of the paper should be blotted off before printing.

An unsized paper should only be damped by sponging, as it easily falls apart and handling it in water can be disastrous. If you should need proof of this try picking a large sheet of blotting paper out of a tray of water – the effect is similar!

As hands become dirty from inking and wiping it is best to handle all papers with paper or card 'fingers'.

Inking

Inking is best done with a generously inked roller on to a warmed plate. Do not have the plate so hot that it cannot be handled easily. (If you do not have a hotplate, add some thin oil to the ink to make it flow more freely.) The heat helps to loosen the stiffish ink, making it easier for inking and wiping. Plates can also be inked with a leather dabber (not recommended for drypoints) or

ETCHING AND ENGRAVING

1. Inking the plate using card.

2. Wiping plate.

3. Laying paper.

4. Printing first plate.

5. Laying down registration in blocks.

6. Inserting second plate.

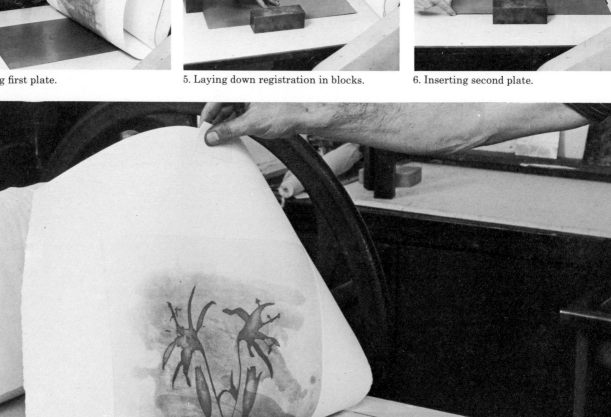

7. Revealing final print.

The final print.
Tiger Lily.
Coloured etching 20″ × 30″
John Henn.

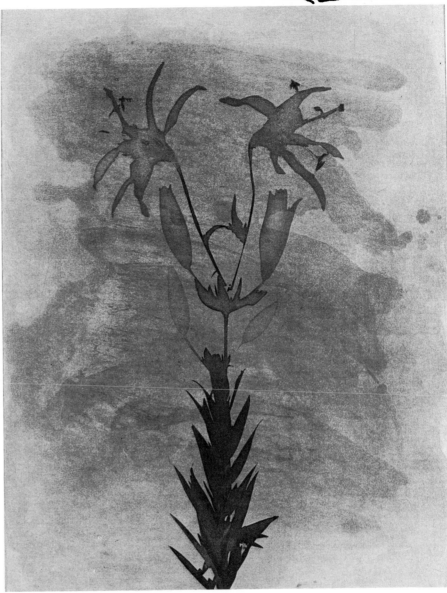

squeegy – a piece of cut card or rubber with which you spread the ink. Work the ink into the lines with a piece of tarleton rolled into a firm ball. Use a fresh piece each day as this stops possible scratching of the plate when the ink has dried on it from previous printings. Most tarleton as supplied by the manufacturer is too stiff with dressing and I like to rub a little of this out before starting to print. It can also be rinsed through and dried on the hotplate. Form a pad but avoid making it too tight or ragged as this defeats its purpose which is to pick up the ink off the surface. When printing, I generally have two or three pads which I use in rotation, the inkiest one first, to remove most of the surplus ink then graduating to cleaner pads.

Wipe the plate with a circular motion starting at the edges and working into the centre. As you firmly rotate the pad it will start to pick up the ink, and as it becomes sticky refold it to present a cleaner face.

The idea is to ink and print only what has been etched and that quality will not be seen if it has been decided to leave extraneous amounts of ink on the surface of the plate because it looked good at the time.

After the final rag (tarleton) wipe, it is usually best to handwipe. This has the effect of sharpening the overall quality by picking up ink left by the rag wipe. When hand wiping keep the hand open and use only the fleshy parts. There is no need to apply pressure. Hands should be wiped clean frequently with a clean rag. Rubbing a little whiting on to your hand will help keep it dry, but any excess whiting which falls on to the plate will dry out the ink giving a patchy print. Some people use paper and tissue instead of hand wiping but I do not believe it is comparable to good, old-fashioned skin, as it soaks up the ink giving a dry, thin looking print. There are, however, occasions when paper and tissue will be useful, especially where the etched lines are very deep. If you must use paper, keep it flat and not in a ball.

A loose ink, that is with added thin oil, inked warm will print with considerably more tone than a plate inked in a stiff ink printed cold.

The first print taken may suffer from broken lines or areas. This could be because the ink was not worked into the crevasses sufficiently. Inking in the same way will start a build-up of ink in the plate and often the second print will be much richer than the first. If the plate continues to print badly, try adding some thin oil to the ink as it could be that the ink is too stiff. Do not clean the plate out between prints with solvent except in some cases of multi-plate colour printing (see below). The plate is cleaned at the end of the printing session and must be left completely dry. It is possible to leave the inked plate for a few hours before printing, but unless in an emergency I see no reason for doing this.

Taking a print
When the inking process is complete lay the inked plate on the bed of the press on top of a sheet of tissue paper to keep the bed and paper clean. Do not use newsprint which will crease because of the damped printing paper and will in turn crease the print. Handling paper is made easier by holding it in diagonally opposite corners. Place the paper down on the plate and smooth the blankets out along the paper. It remains only to roll the bed through the press and peeling the print off slowly from one corner will reveal all. You can erase any slight grubby marks on the paper by dabbing lightly with a water-sodden sponge. The water will not harm the print.

If the print creases check the pressure, if this is satisfactory check the paper to ensure that it is not too dry or too wet. If the ink has bled out of the deep lines, then stiffen up the ink by adding more pigment.

Drying the print
If it is a stage or colour proof then tape down the edges with paper gum strip 5 cm (2 in) wide on to a stiff board, making sure the gum strip is well stuck down. Taping is quick and useful for one or two prints, it will, however, stretch heavily embossed works. The finished prints or edition should be covered with a sheet of tissue and dried between sheets of blotting paper under weights. Again people differ in how they organise their print drying, but basically the idea is to sandwich the prints between two pieces of blotting paper and apply evenly distributed weight. Split the prints into packs of five separated by sheets of hardboard with finally a sheet of block board on which the weights should be placed.

The blotting paper is changed everyday for a week, after which time your print should have dried flat; the ink may still be wet as it takes longer than the paper to dry so be careful when handling the print.

Heavily embossed prints should be allowed to dry without weights then re-soaked and dried normally. This is done to protect the embossment which could be reduced if weight is applied directly after printing. Putting paper that has been re-soaked or sponged clean directly between the drying blotters will cause the blotters to wrinkle, if a weight is then placed on top this wrinkle is transferred to the print. This would mean re-soaking and drying again with fresh dry blotters. Heavily inked prints will also need to dry out naturally first to stop the ink off-setting on to the blotting paper through the protective tissue.

Colour printing
Once the drawing plate is completed, take a print in the usual way, but instead of winding the paper completely through the press and removing it,

catch the end under the roller and throw back the blankets and the caught print over the roller. Before removing the plate, lay down two heavy steel registration blocks along two adjacent sides. The key plate is then removed and a clean plate of the same size is put in its place, the blocks are removed and the print and blankets laid down again. The print and the new plate are run back through the press and the image is off-set on to the second plate. Repeat the process for a third and fourth plate as necessary. The plates are now registered with the first or key plate. Lightly drypoint in the design as a guide, then work into the plate using any of the intaglio methods, remember that each plate will be printed in a different colour and can be used to give four or five or more colours when overprinted.

The plates are then inked for printing in their separate colours. The first is wound through the press and the end of the paper caught under the roller. The blocks are placed beside the first plate which is removed; the second colour plate is registered against the blocks which are then taken away. The paper and blankets are laid down and wound through the press, the print picking up the second colour. This process is repeated for any other colour plates until finally the drawing or key plate is registered and printed.

Usually the lighter colours are printed first and the dark colours and the key plate last, as light colours do not print successfully over dark colours. However, if you do need to print a light colour in a dark area, for instance a yellow spot on a black ball, you must accommodate for the yellow in the black. To do this when making the black plate either stop out the area before etching or scrape away the area with a scraper/burnisher, which allows the yellow undercolour to show through.

It is also advisable to give the colours a slightly different consistency to each other to avoid rejection when overprinting, thus the first plate should have a stiff ink, the second slightly oily, and the third oilier still.

No more than four plates can be successfully printed in this way as the paper dries out each time it passes under the roller.

FURTHER TECHNIQUES

Engraving
Like drypointing there are no acids or grounds involved when engraving. It is a direct and very precise medium. A burin and not a needle is used and by pushing it through the copper it gouges out a line from which a spiral of metal is displaced. This spiral must be cut off using the flat side of a scraper. The strength of the line depends on the size and shape of the burin, i.e. square or lozenge shape and the depth at which you allow it to cut. Engraving directly on to the polished copper may prove difficult because of its shiny surface. This problem can be eased slightly by making sure you work in a diffused but good light reducing the glare that causes eye strain. Another method is to apply a hard ground and lightly draw in the design which is

Engraving tools.

Three square burr trimmer.

Hand trimmer showing different widths.

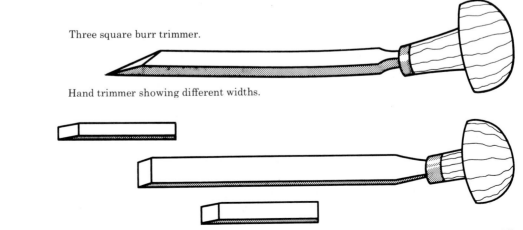

ETCHING AND ENGRAVING

then engraved with the burin.

Holding the burin is done by placing it on the table and picking it up with the handle resting in the palm of the hand, the thumb and forefinger being used for direction only and not for pushing. The ideal place for the thumb and first finger is approximately 5 cm (2 in) behind the cutting face of the tool. Some engravers like to have the first finger on top of the burin for extra pressure and direction is controlled by the thumb and middle finger. Use the

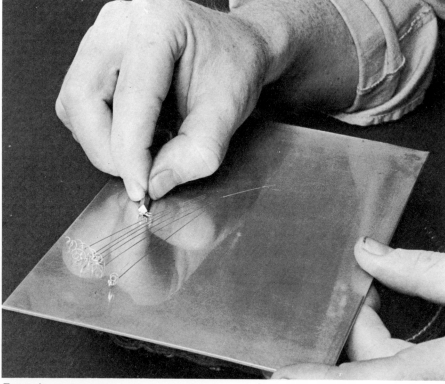

Engraving on to copper.

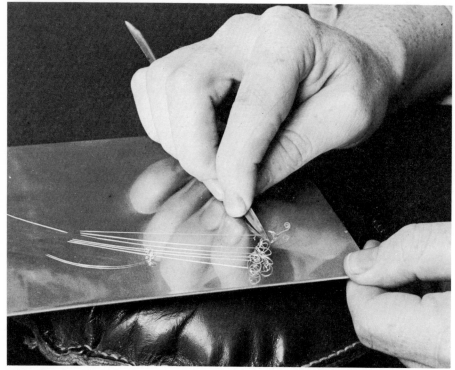

Removing the spiral of copper.

one most comfortable to you. If the burin enters the copper at too shallow an angle it will skid along the surface leaving a fine scratch; if it enters at too steep an angle it will become impossible to move any further. With practice it will become obvious which is the most satisfactory angle of entry. Ideally one should sit alongside the table with your legs and the burin parallel with the edge. The plate should rest on something which allows it to be turned easily – I use a leather covered sandbag. Turning the plate is needed when making a curve instead of turning your arm, and the burin should be banked slightly. Do not get your free hand in front of the burin in case it slips. Your reactions will not be fast enough to prevent an accident. When cutting it is best to keep your head directly above the cutting point of the burin at all times. Remember to push with the heel or butt of the hand and not with the fingers, the main driving force coming from the shoulder – so keep your wrist and arm still. When removing the spiral you must cut in the direction of the line. The burin and the scraper must be kept extremely sharp and may need sharpening many times during a session, the idea being to keep the face of the burin flat. Place the cutting face of the burin on to the sharpening stone and keeping it from rocking by holding it close to the end grind it in a circular motion. Then run the bottom two sides of the shank along the stone to remove the burr that occurs when sharpening the face. A new burin will will need to be sharpened before use.

Before printing you will be able to feel a burr along the engraved line which has to be removed by polishing with fine emery paper or crocus powder, finished off with a metal polish.

If the lines appear broken during printing try using a thinner mix of ink by adding some thin oil. Do make sure the ink is well mulled. You may also need a little more pressure when printing.

Mezzotint

A mezzotint is to work the surface of a copper plate with a serrated tool called a rocker which when inked will print a rich velvet black. The rocker acts as a drypoint needle and forces the metal to sit on the surface and to collect the ink. Using a scraper and burnisher (see below) the idea is to flatten these burrs so they will hold less ink and appear lighter. In mezzo-tinting you are working from black to white. Working or rocking the plate is a methodical and time-consuming process so you will need to be patient.

If attempting a mezzotint try a small plate first. Divide the plate into horizontal lines about 2·5 cm (1 in) apart, and using enough pressure to kick up a burr rock the tool from side to side while slowly moving up the plate. Once you have reached the top move on to the next line and complete in that direction, and continue over the whole plate. Then mark lines at 90° to the previous lines and repeat the rocking process. Again repeat the process on lines marked at 45° and finally make two further divisions and repeat the rocking. When completed the plate should print black.

Print as for a drypoint, being particularly careful of the sensitive and fragile burr. The ink should be mixed with thick oil and should be slightly runny. After inking wipe carefully with a soft tarleton rag to work the ink into the plate then handwipe only. Cotton buds are useful to bring up small light areas.

Photo-etching

Kodak printed resist (KPR) is a liquid photo sensitive acid resist. It is used with KPR Developer and Dye. It is sensitive to ultra-violet light. Over the years of using KPR I have met many artists who vary its control and appli-cation – an advertisement for the flexibility of the material. Below are two methods of application.

(1) Flow coating

Degrease the plate with ammonia and whiting and dry it on the hotplate. Hold the plate underneath to prevent fingermarks, then tipping the plate pour the resist on one edge and let it run quickly down the plate, the excess

Untitled.
Etching lithograph 32″ × 50″
Julian Watmough.

should be allowed to drain into a reservoir to be poured back into the bottle. The plate is stood on its edge to drain. Drying takes 45 minutes to an hour. As thin a coat as possible is needed so do not be tempted to recover missed areas.

(2) Whirling

Hunter Penrose sell a rubber suctioned whirler which is attached to the plate. The resist is poured into the centre of the plate and spun. The centrifugal force spreads it over the plate. Old record players can be adapted for this. The plate is then left to dry.

Exposure

The photograph must be a transparent positive not a negative and must be the same size as the proposed image. It is placed in contact with the coated plate and sellotaped securely. Remember to turn the positive over, this will ensure that the image is printed the right way round.

How long should exposure take? This depends upon the amount and strength of the ultra-violet bulbs used. A test plate will therefore be necessary. I use a graphoscreen containing four 125 watt mercury vapour bulbs fixed at 50 cm (20 in) from the plate. Exposure will take about five to six minutes. After exposure, remove the positive and develop the plate for one minute returning the developer to the pan. Wash the plate under a spray of warm water to wash away the areas of resist which have not been affected by the light, that is the areas which were blocked by the black parts of the

positive. Pour on a little dye and rinse again, the image should be clearly visible. Remove the plate to a hot plate and leave for ten to fifteen minutes to ensure that the resist is dry and hard. If a tone is wanted an aquatint should be laid at this point, but the flame should be kept low to avoid scorching the resist. Finally varnish the unwanted areas of the image and the underside of the plate and etch. After etching, the normal solvents such as meths and white spirit will not remove the resist. Proofs can be taken with the resist on, but before editioning the resist should be taken off with lacquer-type thinners.

Problems
If the resist washes away when rinsing the plate, make sure that when you repeat the process the coating is very thin and is left to dry thoroughly. Repeat the test plate if necessary to establish the correct exposure times.

ERASING & POLISHING

The scraper/burnisher has two roles to play in etching. One is to erase or remove unwanted marks and the other is to use it in a positive and creative manner by scraping into etched or aquatinted areas introducing new shapes and values.

The scraper is a tri-edged tool, having an excellent cutting capability with all metals. When working from black to white to create a new shape, it is best to start with a light pressure which increases as you continue. The reason for this is that the action of the scraper will leave marks in the metal which will print. The scraping is a one-way action only, towards you, the return stroke lifting clear of the plate. The burnisher, on the other hand, is a polishing tool, and will not do the job of a scraper.

When erasing, if a large area is scraped away then snakestone is used to remove the scraper marks that are left. Snakestones come in various sizes and should be prepared for use on an old plate, smoothing and rounding off the sharp edges which could otherwise scratch the plate. Use the snakestones with water to improve their cutting power. After snakestones, charcoal bricks are used to polish away the snakestone marks. Charcoal is used with either meths or oil. Finally, polish with a metal polish such as Brasso to produce a good shine. Wire wool used with a little oil applied with a circular motion is also very good for shining up a plate.

The burnisher is used in conjunction with the scraper, particularly for areas too small for the snakestone. The burnisher must be kept well polished; the scraper needs to be kept sharp by placing a flat edge of the scraper on the sharpening stone and grinding gently in a forward/back motion.

Another method of erasing is to bite away areas of aquatints with acid. First of all I restrict the area of bite using stop-out varnish. I then lay the plate in the acid and using a soft household brush, gently brush the area. Brushing speeds up the process of biting and flattens the 'bumps' of the aquatint reducing the ink-holding qualities considerably.

STORING PLATES

Finally, a word about storing finished plates so that all your hard work is not spoilt. To store a plate for any length of time I degrease the surface with ammonia and whiting and apply a hard ground, making sure that the plate is completely dry. I then wrap it in acid-free tissue and store in a drawer away from damp.

Some printers oil or grease their plates then seal them in wax paper. I find this to be unsatisfactory as the oil and grease do dry out after a period and allow the greaseproof paper to attack the surface of the plate. Blotting paper is also unsatisfactory as it attracts damp.

RELIEF PRINTING

RELIEF PRINTING

RELIEF PRINTING EXPLOITS the surface characteristics of almost any material. Traditionally, these particular characteristics have come from the gouging, cutting or carving out of the surface of a wood block, be it fine or coarse grained. During the 1960s, however, artists and students alike experimented widely, expanding the concept of a 'relief' print and discovered a whole host of new and often unprinted imagery. Great emphasis was placed on the 'found' object or material and on the inclusion of natural surfaces, such as corroded metal, eroded wood, into prints. Some artists even went as far as casting in rubber latex to record the surface of an object. Print 'assemblages' became the norm in which disparate elements were inked up and brought together in one work.

One of the main advantages of the relief print, besides the scope it offers for very wide and creative use, is that there is no major processing to go through before printing begins, apart from cutting or making the block. It is probably the most direct of all the printing methods, the fastest and possibly the easiest in the technical sense and good results can be obtained with or without a press. It is the most direct of all the printing processes as the paper is placed on top of the block and a print taken without any intermediate or offset rollers or machinery. It is possibly the fastest of all the print processes and in its simplest form the stamping of an inked block on a piece of paper will create an image, and that could be said to be the easiest of all the printing techniques with variations made to suit the printer! Good results can be obtained with or without a press, although in its finest and most delicate form some type of even pressure is necessary.

RELIEF PRINTING WITHOUT A PRESS

Materials and equipment

Very few materials need to be bought for the simpler forms of relief printing. Crayons are needed for rubbings but need not necessarily be of a special kind although for connoisseurs, special rubbing sticks are manufactured. Either oil or water based inks can be used and the consistency must be quite tacky in both cases otherwise the inks will run into the lower areas of the block or object and blur the printed image. A small rubber or gelatine roller is useful for careful and controlled inking of a surface and depending on the nature of the print required either a hard or soft roller should be chosen. A hard roller will ink simply the very top surface, a softer roller will ink a little more of the upper surfaces.

An even, clean, flat surface is necessary to roll the ink film out on to – a piece of glass, perspex or formica is the best. Cleaning rags, liquids, newsheet and a bin are essential and a table (or firm surface) covered with papers is probably necessary to work on.

In the majority of cases of making a relief print the printing paper comes into direct contact with the block or object. This means that the resulting image will be a mirror image or reversal of the block and it is important to consider this aspect before setting out on any blockmaking preparations. If the image for a block has been taken from a drawing, then the block must be made in reverse so that the image will print correctly.

Something that can not be described as either 'materials' or 'equipment' is a tidy approach to working and is essential otherwise chaos will result. Be fairly strict and if you have spilt any ink or find yourself getting ink up your arms, stop, clean up and start again. This is not a process that will suffer greatly for a pause of five minutes or so – unlike screen printing where a break of even a couple of minutes will cause many printing problems.

Printing

Applying enough pressure to a surface (the paper or block) to make the print is quite easy, the main problem to be solved is that of keeping the paper and block together whilst applying the pressure – a shift will cause the image to

Spooning to obtain relief print.

smudge and the lines will become unsharp. Most prints are taken with the paper placed on top of the inked object or block. Pressure can be applied on to the paper in a variety of ways: with the palm of the hand, with a wooden spoon, or with a barren (a soft circular polishing disc covered with either leather, cloth or bamboo leaves). In all cases, the action must be positive, starting from the middle and working systematically outwards. Again, a circular motion is probably the easiest way of achieving an even print. The paper can be held carefully in place with one hand whilst the other is used to make the print, or weights can be placed at the corners of the sheet and the printing takes place after the sheet is gently lowered on top. Even drawing pins can be used to pin the paper in position but the holes will remain on the print!

With the majority of blocks and objects in this particular section, it is necessary to take a proof to decide the correct consistency required for the ink, the right pressure to put on the block when printing and the correct paper to choose to print on to. If the print is not quite right, thicken or loosen the ink up, press harder or softer with the inking roller, press harder or softer with the burnishing spoon (a clean, dry roller can even be used to print with). Make lots of experiments until you have exactly the image you need from your printing block – it may even be necessary to clean the block occasionally as a build up of ink can occur, again causing blurring of the image.

Papers

The choice of a printing paper is always personal and varies greatly with the required effect of the printed image. However, in the relief printing process, it is probably wise to choose a fairly absorbent paper, that is a paper without much size in it. With an absorbent paper the ink sinks immediately to the lower layers of the sheet of paper and when taking an image from an object or block this is more desirable for a better record of the image. In heavily sized papers, the ink remains on the surface of the sheet (best seen in lithography and screen printing) and if the block has not been perfectly inked up a blurring of the image will result due to overloading of the ink. Examples of more absorbent papers are newsheet, filter and blotting papers, waterleaf handmade papers and Japanese papers.

65

Corrugated paper.

Crumpled tracing paper.

Feather.

Plastic webbing.

Some of the effects that can be achieved using common, every day objects and materials, by simple stamp printing.

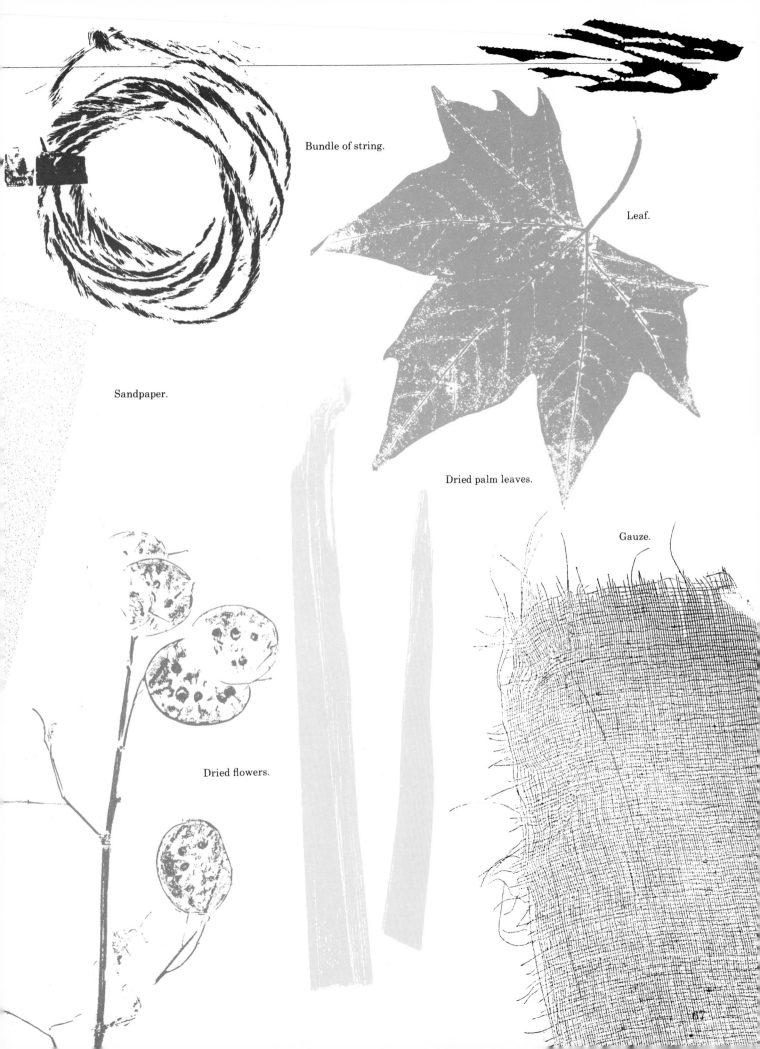

Bundle of string.

Leaf.

Sandpaper.

Dried palm leaves.

Gauze.

Dried flowers.

RELIEF PRINTING

Inks and drying times

Water based inks will dry faster than oil based inks but an oil based ink will probably give better definition to a block or object. It is advisable to leave a print to dry for twenty-four hours before printing again on the same sheet when using oil based inks. However, a tissue paper mask can be laid over wet images whilst another part of the image is printed but only if great care is taken.

Types of print

In making a relief print, ink is generally applied to the top or the uppermost surface of a block (or object) and it is this surface that will give the printed image. In this section the initial work is in finding a surface that you wish to print from – anything can be used from a wooden bench, a crushed egg box to a telephone dial or printed circuit.

(1) Frottage

Probably the easiest of all methods which fit into the relief printing bracket is 'frottage' or rubbings. A sheet of reasonably thin paper such as newsheet or tracing paper (or at its best, a thin Japanese paper) is placed then held either with hand or weights over the object. With a light, circular motion, a wax crayon is carefully rubbed over the surface and will pick up the image from the top surface of the object below. Rubbings demand no particular skill, simply a little care and patience.

(2) Stamp printing

Direct prints from any surface can be taken by inking up the surface and pressing it on to paper or pressing the paper on to it. A stamp print is always made with a kiss and can especially be viewed as such when lipstick is used. Another easily identifiable image is that of a hand print in which the palm of the hand (or even other parts of the body) has been rolled up with ink and pressed directly on to the paper. Natural surfaces such as leaves, feathers, wood, all give splendid images of themselves, making one aware of characteristics that previously may not have been noticed.

Stamp printing itself takes its name from the action of the stamp and anything can be stamped, from the impression of a tyre wheel, the rim of a pot, to specially manufactured rubber stamps. These are used in offices and banks for a number of purposes; a tin containing an inked pad is readily supplied and a quick stamp and bang provides information in the form of a print on many official documents. The same principle can be utilised in many other ways to make one's own images.

(3) Block making

The world of the printing block is enormous with every conceivable piece of collaged material able to be used. At its simplest, plain glue such as PVA or Copydex can be spread on to a piece of hardboard or cardboard, and patterns made into it with a comb, pin, or any serrated edge. When it is dry, the surface is inked up and a print taken which emulates the characteristics of the glue or paste utilised.

Images can be made by cutting out shapes in card, corrugated card or paper and sticking them firmly in place on the block base before printing takes place. Even collages of many different types of material can be arranged on one block – string, paper clips, pins, milk bottle tops, lace, etc. and printed to give different textures to one particular image. Care must be taken with a collaged block. Great differences in levels on the block will not help to make a good print, so objects with a similar height and depth must be chosen. Loose material will be picked up by the inking roller and so everything must be very firmly stuck down. It is often advisable, when making blocks of any type, to roll a thin film of ink over the top surface and let it dry. This then soaks in and seals the surface and facilitates future printing, also giving an indication of how the final printed image will look.

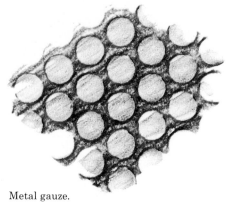

Metal gauze.

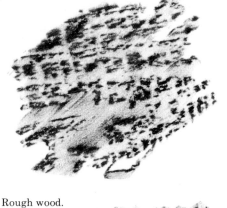

Rough wood.

Reverse side of linoleum.

Concrete.

Above: Examples of simple rubbings using a wax crayon and thin paper.

Right: Linocut. Rama Khalid (student).

RELIEF PRINTING

Relief printing press.

(4) Roller prints (offset printing)

If an extremely delicate or very detailed impression is required of a complicated object such as a feather, piece of fur or of a hard object with varying levels such as a pair of scissors or a clothes peg, a roller print can be made in which such details as required can be reproduced. Two soft gelatine rollers are required for this type of printing; one to ink the object and the other to make the print. A layer of thin ink is rolled out first and the object carefully inked up avoiding overloading any of the details with ink. The clean roller is then carefully pressed over the inked object and an impression is gained on the roller which is then pressed out on to the printing paper. This is called 'offset' printing. In this particular method care should be taken to choose an 'offset' roller that has a large enough diameter to cover the whole object in one roll, and when printing, care should be taken not to press too hard otherwise the image will be distorted on the sheet. This is actually the only method in the relief printing field in which the image can be printed the correct way round due to the insertion of an offset roller in the printing process.

RELIEF PRINTING WITH A PRESS

Presses

Although it is possible to print quite effectively using only a wooden spoon or barren, a printing press provides an evenness to the printed image that is not often found in hand work and for printing on a large scale (both actual size and edition size) it is a necessity.

The history of relief printing presses dates back well into the fifteenth century when the demand for printed matter of all kinds exploded and a method (other than by hand) had to be found to produce newspapers and books at a faster rate. Early presses were large, cumbersome, wooden contrivances that exerted a downward force on to wooden type below. Presses have had various modifications but the best relief presses still maintain the same action – that of an even downward pressure on to the paper below. In the early nineteenth century a large ornate iron press superseded the wooden one and as simultaneous developments took place both in Britain and America the Albion Press (or the Columbian in America) took precedence over most of its rivals. Built to last and in a variety of sizes, these presses provided excellent printing qualities and although they are not manufactured today, reconditioned they are worth seeking out. They were made in a large number of bed sizes, mainly related to book sizes; some being 'table' models, others weighing over 200 kg (4 cwt). Trade printers obviously regard the Albion as obsolete but for the artist or amateur printer they are a treasure.

The platen and the bed form the two main distinct parts of the Albion Press. The bed holds the inked blocks and printing paper on top. The bed is moved under the platen which when lowered comes into direct contact with whatever is on the bed and with the pressure creates the print.

It is important that the bed is moveable as once a print is made the blocks must be removed and re-inked for the next print. To facilitate this, the bed is mounted on a carriage which runs along two rails and by means of unwinding and winding a girth, using a rounce handle, the bed moves laterally backwards and forwards.

At the end of the bed is hinged a tympan. This is a metal frame covered with parchment or linen which is lowered on top of the bed holding the sandwich of block, paper and press packing together whilst the pressure is exerted. The tympan disc governs the thickness of the packing and acts as a cover for the bed whilst the metal platen is lowered.

The pressure from the Albion is exerted by means of a knuckle joint operating from a hollow piston from which the platen is suspended. When a print is made the platen is forced down by the action of pulling on a lever. An

RELIEF PRINTING

even downward pressure is exerted on to the paper below. A certain expertise is necessary to use this press correctly and well. The platen handle must reach 'home' each time a print is made and so the press packing (see p. 84) and bed must be adjusted to suit the type of work being printed.

If not undertaken in the correct manner, taking a print from a large Albion or Columbian press can cause physical strain, especially to the back. Many press users place one leg on the guiderails to help pull home the platen, but the best method uses a large wooden block sited directly under the bed guide rails. The wooden block acts as a rest for the feet so that the whole body can be thrown into pulling the press.

Many other types of presses can be used quite effectively to make a relief print and many ingenious devices have been invented. The main point to be remembered must be that the print is being taken from a raised, top surface and so other types of presses from the various print processes are unsuitable. Bookbinders screw down presses are splendid and can be found in sale rooms or printer's auctions or even in the 'For Sale' columns of art magazines.

As the relief press was invented for wood blocks and type, the trade has gone on to many more sophisticated, fast-running kinds of presses but in their wake have left behind small proofing letter press machines, such as the Stephenson Blake small proofing press, which is hand operated with automatic inking rollers and which will provide an admirable printing press for anyone wishing to print small editions.

Siting of presses

Because of the weight of many of the Albion/Columbian presses it is advisable to site them with care and attention. A ground or basement floor, concrete if possible, is best or if not 'spreaders' – 5×10 cm (2×4 in) planks of timber – must be placed under the feet of the press and at 90° to floor joists to spread the load of the weight.

Tools

In the traditional manner, making a relief print necessitates that marks and gouges are cut out of a block. The areas that remain on the top surface of the block will create the image. But because the process is one of direct printing contact, as already mentioned any impression taken directly from the block will be reversed. This should be kept in mind when planning any cutting work.

(1) Gouges and knives

These are the basic tools for cutting both lino and wood blocks. Gouges vary in size from small 'V' shaped tools, called 'viners' or 'scrivers' which are used mainly for making fine lino cuts, to large 'U' shaped tools used mainly for clearing out small areas and backgrounds. Various handles exist for the tools; the best are either lozenge or pear shaped and the tool must be held with the handle fitting snugly into the palm of the hand.

Cutting should always take place away from the body, as accidents in which the tool slips can be lethal. For right-handed people the cutting action is often in a diagonal line to the left and vice versa for left-handed cutters. The block is easily turned as the direction of the cutting indicates, and to facilitate this turning a small leather filled sandbag is often placed underneath the block, so that it is centrally balanced and will pivot easily.

Knives have been the traditional tool for the oriental woodblock artists for centuries but almost any knife (such as a scalpel) will make a cut or gouging mark into a block. The Japanese hold their knives like a dagger and the cutting is done so that the line (or area) left for printing is narrower at the surface than at the base of the cut. This means that the cutting edge of the blade is always closest to the block.

A 'multiple' tool is employed to cut a series of fine lines in one stroke but it is obvious that in this method any tool that will scratch, dent, cut or mark the surface can be used to build up a multitude of textures – a nail, a pin, a serrated edge of any kind will all mark the block, even the pounding of a

hammer on a wooden surface will create a ripple texture. Ordinary carpenter's tools work well on all types of wooden blocks – electric sanders, jigsaws, etc., although it may be necessary to clamp large blocks to a firm surface before attempting any specially 'creative' work!

Sharpening gouges and knives
Gouges and knives are sharpened in a very careful and controlled manner on an 'India' or 'Carborundum' stone with oil and then on an 'Arkansas' or 'Washita' for greater keenness. The sharpening of all tools needs practice, especially that of a hollow tool. A slip stone, with a wedge-shape at one side for the 'V' tools and a rounded edge at the other for 'U' tools is used to sharpen the insides of hollow gouges and mainly to remove the burr which is caused by pressing the bevel on the outside edge of the tool on the slip stone. The 'V' tool must be sharpened on two edges alike holding the bevel surface flat against the stone and moving in an elliptical sphere using plenty of oil. For very large cutting tools, it is probably preferable to rub the stone against the tool instead of vice versa.

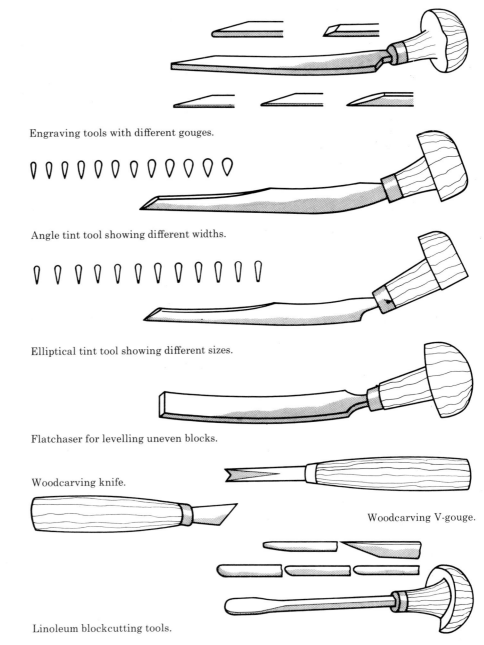

Engraving tools with different gouges.

Angle tint tool showing different widths.

Elliptical tint tool showing different sizes.

Flatchaser for levelling uneven blocks.

Woodcarving knife.

Woodcarving V-gouge.

Linoleum blockcutting tools.

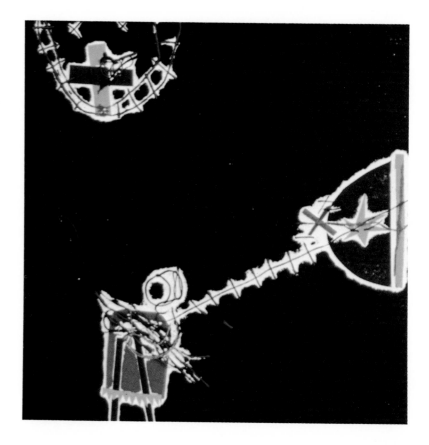

Illustration to a song.
Lino, paper, string and ink 41″ × 41″
Martin McGinn.

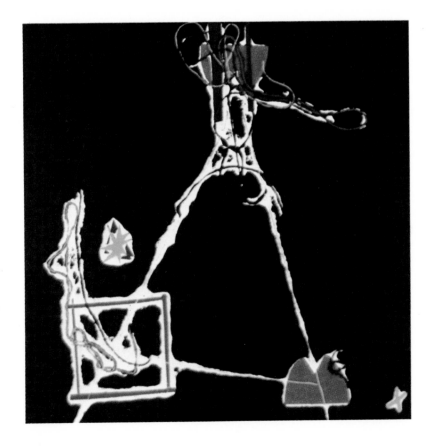

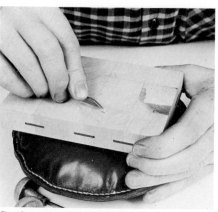

Cutting out wood engraving block.

Inking up block.

Burnishing to transfer image.

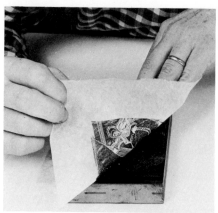

Revealing print.

(2) Engraving tools

Making an engraving on to an end block necessitates quite a different technique to cutting, and utilises a different set of tools of a much finer and precise nature. As in the woodcut, the engraver's cutting gesture is away from the body but exerted in a more controlled and skilled manner. An assortment of burins are used to engrave into the block in various shapes and sizes, and unlike the 'V' and 'U' section gouges, they do not gouge out areas, but simply lift different types of small, thin lines from the block. These are classified under the names of 'lozenge' tools (or standard graver), spit-stickers (or tint tools), scorpers (or gravers) and multiple line tools.

It is essential to keep these tools clean and sharp and a serious engraver will keep a sharpening kit with his or her tools. Resharpening must be carefully controlled by holding the tool close to its edge against the sharpening stone and moving it in an elliptical motion, keeping the face of the tool flat. An India stone with light oil is first used and the finishing done on an Arkansas hardstone.

Blocks

The requirements for wood block cutting and engraving are very simple and any workshop or studio can be quickly arranged to suit personal requirements. The three main areas of work are – cutting, printing, inking and cleaning areas. The work-table or bench for cutting the blocks needs to be sturdy and well organised, close to a good natural or artificial light source and at best height for sitting or bending for long periods at a time.

(1) Woodcut blocks

The woodcut is worked on the plank grain of almost any piece of wood. It is cut with 'V', 'U' and any other relevant tools and is normally from soft woods such as pine. Many artists have simply enhanced the natural grain of the plank of wood by rubbing stiffly with a wire brush. The woodcutting technique in general is used for large work, often encompassing more gestural and dynamic marks.

It is advisable if you are going to work with a press to try and achieve a block height of about 2·2 cm (approx. $\frac{7}{8}$ in) which is the height most presses are built for. Having completed the drawing in reverse on the plank, the areas which are to remain white (or unprinted) must be cut away, but it is often difficult on a complicated cut to see exactly what you are doing and whether you are cutting deep enough. It is wise (and by the way most interesting) to take proofs at several stages in your cutting to make sure that the image is progressing correctly. The black ink left on the block after cleaning acts as a good base into which the new marks can clearly be seen.

Far left: Woodcut: Andrew Davidson.

(2) Wood engraving blocks

If your work requires close, precise and detailed cutting or engraving, then this is done on the end grain of the wood. It is even grained, free of knots and probably a hard wood. Engravings have been traditionally made on apple, pear and box wood but others such as oak, maple and chestnut can be used. The blocks are bought in any size, although largish blocks are composed of smaller blocks joined together. The blocks are made type-high, approx. 2·2 cm (about $\frac{7}{8}$ in), and highly polished on one surface only. These blocks can be resurfaced once used but obviously will have less depth.

Preliminary drawings can be transferred on to the block either by using a carbon paper or by rubbing Indian ink into the surface and scraping into that. Once cutting begins, remember that what is left on the block will print and that a one line cut will leave a white line on the image; to achieve a black line, both sides of the line must be cut away. The Japanese first make their preliminary drawings in Indian ink on to very fine tissue-like paper and then paste it face downwards with flour paste on to the block and cut straight through the tissue into the block. In this way there is no difficulty reversing the image.

Painting image on lino.

(3) Lino block

The cost of making a lino cut is very low and even when it is set type high for easier use in a press, the price is minimal compared to the cost of plates from other processes. Its qualities are quite different from either plank or end grain wood but nevertheless, used well can produce quite remarkable results.

Almost any type of lino can be used but the best is about 0·95 cm (about $\frac{3}{8}$ in) deep and has a canvas backing. It should be plain in colour so that marks can easily be seen and kept flat if at all possible. Rolling the lino may induce cracking. If the surface is a little rough scraping with a razor blade will even out the lumps or bumps. For easier cutting the lino should be warmed over a radiator, a sharp tool will then slide through the surface. All the tools that are used for wood cutting and engraving can be used effectively on lino although they may lose their sharpness due to grit in the lino. As soon as you feel that the tool has lost its 'key' or 'edge' it must be resharpened.

Cutting out image.

(4) Hardboard block

Hardboard is also a cheap and practical material to use as a block, although often forms the base for a collage-type work (see p. 68). It is possibly a little thin in depth to be used with great dexterity but with imaginative use can be most impressive.

(5) Plywood block

Plywood obtained from tea chests is probably too thin to be of much use to the block cutter but thicker plywood can provide an interesting source of texture. Plywood is a very stable block making material and the Japanese use the very refined surface of *katsura* on many of their wood blocks. Plywood is often used for jigsaw cutting; that is large areas of shaped blocks which are inked up separately and re-assembled before printing takes place (see p. 81).

(6) Card block

Good quality thick card is also a most useful material. Again mainly in use for the jigsaw technique it provides a cheaper and easier-to-cut solution than plywood and if treated correctly is capable of printing complex and multi-coloured editions in large numbers (see p. 81).

Inks

Both water and oil based inks are used in relief printing. Water based are mostly used with the easier type of block (e.g. collage block) and are often found in schools where little money is available and where water is the main

RELIEF PRINTING

Welsh canal, Hand coloured linocut, John Woodcock.

Linocut: Uribe (student).

RELIEF PRINTING

cleaning fluid. Oil based inks are preferred and most widely used by professional artists and those who seek to control their work to a finer degree of accuracy. Both tubes and tins (often 0·45 kg/1 lb tins) can be purchased. Tubes are economical and will suffice if not much printing is to be done, cans are essential when editions requiring large amounts of ink are planned. The range of coloured inks is wide and an extender base to reduce the colour to a transparent tint is also available in two forms – 'tinteen' or 'reducing medium'. Metallic colours such as gold, silver, copper, bronze and zinc are made in paste or in powder form. The powder is sprinkled on to an already printed colour and the residue blown off. The paste is probably a better way of printing a metallic colour and contains three separate elements which must be mixed to a fine paste before printing.

The oil based inks can be quite stiff to use and are normally softened by the addition of a little linseed oil. The consistency can be likened almost to soft butter. A spray is available which retards the drying of the ink and can be sprayed on mixed inks and in the cans to prevent a skin forming.

Rollers
Inking rollers are an essential part of the printing outfit and it is important that you purchase the best you can afford. Inking rollers are used to spread a thin and very even film of ink over the block and it is essential that they are kept clean and dust-free the whole of their life. It is normal to have a variety of sizes of rollers for inking various different blocks and very large rollers are essential for large flat areas of colour. Note that the diameter (or circumference) of the roller will be important when inking large blocks and purchase as wide a diameter as possible.

Rollers are made in three types of material: rubber, gelatine and polyurethane, in grades of hard or soft. Hard rollers are used to ink hard, even-surfaced blocks whilst soft ones can put ink into lower parts of the block if necessary. Rubber is the hardest of materials and lasts reasonably but is not perhaps as sensitive as are gelatine or polyurethane rollers.

Gelatine rollers are in common use and are supple and pliable but do not age particularly well and are deteriorated by sunlight, heat and moisture in the air. They are often found fitted into a handle with a removable shaft so that it is easy to take out and replace the worn or damaged roller. Polyurethane rollers have a slightly longer life than gelatine and can be used for most types of work.

Care of rollers
Rollers must never be left to stand in the ink but always left resting on the handle or stood in a rack. As in the case of all tools, rollers must not be left with ink on them to dry. Cleaning ink off should always be done with a soft cloth; scraping the ink with a palette knife will mark the surface and leave an indent that will ruin the inking area of the roller forever. Hooks can be screwed into the handles to allow the rollers to be hung up when in store (in a cupboard preferably) and for large rollers with wooden or metal hand grips at either end a special rack can be constructed to house several at once.

Printing in colour and registration
Any block can be printed in colour. The inking of a block in a single colour completely different to that intended will change and alter the image beyond recognition. However, to print one image in a variety of colours and to repeat the exact colour printing for an edition takes a little planning and forethought. There are various methods of printing and registering colour. Perhaps the easiest is the card or jigsaw type block in which individual pieces are inked up in separate colours and assembled on the bed of the press and the whole thing printed in one printing. More complicated is the cutting and registering of several blocks which are to be printed singly until the final print is obtained and in which it is usual to print an edition of one colour and let it dry to be followed by the next.

Registration is the method used to allow the correct positioning and

An alternative method for making relief prints is by etching the linoleum. The reverse side and edges are painted with PVA liquid plastic to protect the linoleum and prevent false biting. Hot paraffin wax is painted on the surface of the linoleum as either a direct image, or covering the whole area which is then engraved. The linoleum is immersed in a caustic solution (caustic soda and water) which etches into the exposed parts (the strength of the solution determines the depth of etch) leaving the image as a relief.

Applying PVA to back of lino.

Painting on hot wax.

Immersing in caustic solution.

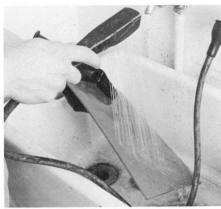
Washing off caustic solution.

Ironing dry.

alignment of various different blocks that make up the image. The registration methods in relief printing cannot compare with the more sophisticated fine line registration of say screen printing methods but nevertheless will produce accurate results.

Registration of a 'jigsaw' block – Method 1

Before the pieces of the jigsaw block are cut a master drawing is made as a plan from which to cut the shapes. This can be used directly on the base of the press, held in position with masking tape and as each piece of card or wood is inked up it is assembled in its relevant place on the master plan. It is probably wise to link the back of each area of wood or card and its corresponding area on the master plan with a number so that if two shapes look alike there will be no mistaking their correct position. Note that in a stanley knife card cut, white lines will separate each area; the shapes of card may meet if a knife with a very thin blade (such as a scalpel) is used. However it still may be necessary to use the second registration method for very accurate printing.

Registration – Method 2

Probably the easiest of all colour registration methods is based on the assumption that all blocks for a certain colour print are of the same size. The printing paper is placed down on to the bed of the press and the block placed in the position required. Obviously when printed it is essential to have at least two outside edges/lines of the block showing and to have each block of the same size. Subsequent colour blocks are inked up and placed face downwards on top and aligned to the block already printed.

Registration – Method 3

The most traditional manner of registering is when separate blocks are used for each colour. In this procedure, a tracing is made from the master drawing for each block to be cut. The blocks are cut individually and printed separately. The main difficulty lies in registering the paper and the block so that each is lined up correctly in the finished print. To do this, it is usual for a 'key' or 'master' block to be cut – one which has the most detail in it or even better a black outline block. When this outline block is cut it is printed in black ink on to several sheets of paper/tracing/acetate. Whilst these are wet, they are run through the press in contact with a new block and so will offset the key block image on to the new block. The colour blocks are then cut separately for the various areas required. The blocks can be cut with each one remaining exactly the same size as the key block, or if only small parts of the block are required, less wastage on the wood/lino occurs if the areas required are trimmed separately. Remember that it is wise to take colour areas under a black outline, i.e. cut them slightly bigger than required.

Before printing begins, a bed plan must be made. A large sheet of thick paper must be taped on the bed of the press and the position of the printing paper marked along one corner and two adjacent sides. Often small rectangles of card are stuck down on to the plan to facilitate the accurate placing of the paper. A key print taken on acetate is useful at this stage. It is placed on the area where the printing paper is to lie and arranged wherever the print is required. One edge (right or left hand) is then taped firmly down. The colour blocks are then printed individually underneath and aligned with the corresponding area of print and a mark is drawn all the way around the outside edge of the block so that as each one is linked up it is placed on the bed of the press in its correct position relative to the printing paper. It is then usual for each colour to be printed before the key block. The key block, inked up in black, is printed last and unites the colour areas.

Registration – Method 4

This method involves little or no actual registration but colour printing takes place in a chance or even haphazard way in which elements of the

Woodcut from plankwood: Haydon Cotton (student).

Woodcuts: Andrew Davidson.

image are inked up and placed at random face down on top of the printing paper. A colour image can be built up in this way from disparate, found objects but not often evenly editioned.

Printing

There are two main stages in the printing operation: proofing and editioning. Proofing entails a print being taken from the block at various stages during the cutting operations to see how the work is progressing and these are termed 'trial proofs' or 'states'. Proofs may be taken just before editioning begins to ascertain the correct consistency of the ink, the correct placing of image on paper, the correct pressure on the press. Editioning is simply the printing of a number of identical prints which match the proof print (BAT) you have chosen as the best colour image.

Quantities of inks, the colours necessary, are mixed up on the inking slab, and a small amount of experience will allow you to do this with ease and certainty. They are rolled out into a thin film. It is normal to print only one colour at a time and traditionally the lightest colour is printed first, the darkest last. Experiments with the inking roller will show that it is possible to produce a blend of several colours on one roller simply by placing individual colours at positions approximately 5 cm (2 in) apart along the inking slab and by running the roller over these with a slight sideways movement, a blend or merge or rainbow effect is achieved. Normally the edition of each colour is printed at one time and hung to dry before subsequent colours are printed. When completed, the remaining ink from one printing can be wrapped up into a small packet in either polythene or greaseproof paper and will keep for several months.

It is most important to 'pack' the press well before printing begins, that is to adjust the packing on the press to suit the block being printed. On most Albion-type presses, the best height for a block is 'type-high' as mentioned above. For thinner blocks, such as card, hardboard, plywood, the bed of the press is packed up with other boards (such as chipboard, hardboard, card) to a suitable height over the whole area of the bed. Minor adjustments to the height of the block can then be made by addition and removal of these boards. The refinements to the press packing are made with paper placed on top of the printing paper. If a sharp print, fine texture or cut line is required, hard top packing is used such as a sheet of thin card. When areas of colour or reliefed blocks are being printed soft top packing is required, such as soft blotting paper, cartridge or filter paper. If the ink is required to be picked up from more than one surface on the block an ordinary blanket or newsheet can be used with heavy pressure. In any case test printing of the block will allow adjustments to be made before the final editioning takes place.

Placing and handling of clean printing paper on the bed or on top of the block is often done with the aid of 'paper fingers', two small strips of folded paper which are used to pick up the paper when your hands are dirty.

Rolling up

Effective inking of a block depends on many factors; the material of the block, the absorbency of the paper, the consistency of the ink, the pressure on the press. Experimentation with all of these aspects is necessary before printing or editioning begins to ascertain the conditions necessary for the best results. The length of the roller's stroke is approximately three times its diameter, after that length it begins a second roll and its ink store is badly depleted having left most of it on the block. To ink any surface successfully takes a great deal of practice with a roller and the larger the area (especially flat areas) the more difficult it becomes. Practice is essential and repeated rollings often in different directions will eventually give an even film to your block. It is important to learn how to roll out an even layer of colour on a flat glass (perspex or laminate) slab and then transfer this film of ink on to the block, replenish the roller and re-ink the block etc. To clean the roller/ink, sprinkle a little turps on to a flat surface and roll the roller through it until the ink is softened then wipe with a soft, clean cloth.

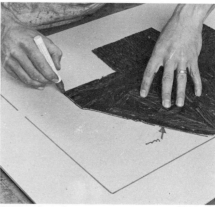

Registering plate.

Inking up.

Inking up block.

Laying plate on press.

Registering paper.

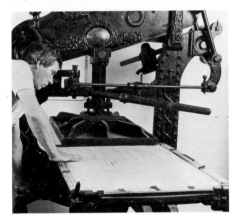

Rolling bed under press.

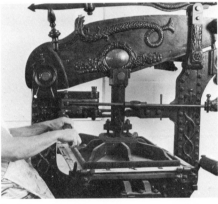

Applying pressure.

Revealing print.

Left: The registering and printing process.

Below:
Woodcut: Andrew Davidson.

Subtraction method of printing

This particular method is quite difficult and relies on the artist's judgement and ability to foresee what might happen to the work over a long period of time. One block only is used and initially the whole block is printed uncut or with a minimum of cut lines. The edition is pulled from this block plus a large number of proofs for test printing. The block is then cut into and parts taken away thus removing areas from the printing surface. A second colour printing is taken directly on top of the first. This procedure is repeated until very small details or areas of the block are left, each time the printing takes place on top of the preceding print.

Cleaning up

As stated at the beginning of this section a tidy approach to work is essential and careful cleaning of materials will save time and money in the long run.

Turpentine substitute is the main cleaning agent for oil based inks although petrol and paraffin can be used. Ink is cleaned off the rollers, palette knives, blocks and inking slabs with a soft cotton rag leaving everything scrupulously clean. Rollers should be hung up when not in use and metal bins should house all the dirty rags and newspapers which have been used in cleaning up operations.

SCREEN PRINTING

SCREEN PRINTING

SCREEN PRINTING IS A PROCESS which is quite different from the other three major printing processes. It is one of the newest of the graphic arts having very little history, its invention dates back to the beginning of this century although its predecessor, the stencil, has a much longer history. It is a planographic process, like lithography, in that it lays down a very flat layer of colour, but this layer can be applied to the paper in any thickness, even though the majority of inks today made for the commercial trade are extremely 'thin film'. Rich colours are an added advantage that the screen process has to offer and the widest variety of tints and finishes are available. Glass, metal, plastic, balloons, fabrics, not to mention all types of paper and card are available to the screen printer to use and the relative ease of multicolour printing has made the screen process more and more popular.

Another advantage of this technique is that in its simplest form it requires a minimum of equipment and machinery (which need not be very expensive to set up) and it does not necessarily call for wide technical experience or skills.

The latest popular development in screen printing is that of the photostencil and the use of photography, which is now open to almost anyone to do with ease. Photo-screen printing has progressed at a rapid rate and has allowed much imaginative and inventive work to be made.

EQUIPMENT

The screen frame

A wooden frame must be built or bought to act as a support for the mesh. It must be rigid, square-cornered and well jointed and can be made of either wood or metal. It should be sturdily constructed and when laid on a table remain perfectly flat. A poorly built frame will twist with wear and cause distortion of the mesh, making printing and registration impossible. The size of the screen frame should generally be determined by the type of work to be undertaken. It need not necessarily be square, but it should be of a convenient format for several different sizes of prints. A factor to be considered when determining the size of the frame is the width of the mesh and it is advisable to build (or buy) a frame which uses the mesh economically.

Small ready-made screen frames can be found in various forms, such as a window frame bought from a do-it-yourself shop, which for the beginner provides an easy and cheap solution. However, for the printer wishing to set up her or his own small screen printing operation a stronger, more permanent frame is necessary. These can be bought direct from a screen printing supplier or made at home. To make your own screen frame you will need: four lengths of planed hard wood, nails, hammer, waterproof glue, and varnish or lacquer.

Construction

It is important that the wood chosen for the frame is a good, straight length, dry, preferably seasoned, and knot free. It should be a fairly hard wood but light in weight so that it can be lifted and carried easily. Cedar and beech are the best woods. Deal is more easily available but has a tendency to warp. Choose a wood that is at least 5×5 cm (2×2 in) in diameter and for larger frames, 152×102 cm (60×40 in), use 10×5 cm (4×2 in).

Constructing the corner joints is a most important part of the framemaking, as it is their strength which keeps the screen rigid; there are four basic types which can be used.
(a) Butt joint. This is effective only for smaller size screen frames and should be strengthened with metal corner brackets.
(b) Mitre joint. This should also be strengthened with corner brackets.
(c) Lap joint. An interlocking joint which is secured by screws.
(d) Open bridle or mortice and tenon. This is the firmest joint with least likelihood of warping.

It is very important to cut the joints accurately and it is advisable to work on a flat, firm surface. Each joint must be glued before nailing or screwing together, and the glued joints should be left to dry for twenty-four hours. Finally the outside of the bottom edge of the frame should be rounded off with sandpaper to ease the stretching of the mesh, the rest of the edges being left square and sharp and the whole frame should be given a coat of varnish or lacquer. This stops the ink penetrating into the wood, making it easier to clean, and helps prevent warping.

The mesh

The mesh is stretched very tightly over the base of the screen frame and it is this which acts as a sieve and container for the printing ink. It must be strong, durable and tensile and can be chosen from a variety of fabrics according to one's purse. Usual mesh fabrics include cotton organdie, silk, nylon, terylene and polyester, varying in price from 50p ($1.00) per metre (approx. 40 in) to £10 ($20) per metre.

The mesh is usually sold by a grading scheme dependent on how many threads there are per square centimetre (or square inch). The choice of grading depends upon the type of image to be printed. In general, for large flat areas of colour a coarse/medium grading is required, in which the percentage of open areas in the mesh is large compared to the number of threads, so allowing a greater amount of ink to pass through. A finer fabric will print a very thin deposit of ink and is used to support detailed stencils.

Types of mesh
(a) Cotton organdie: This is the cheapest material to buy and can be easily stretched by hand. It does sag with frequent use but can easily be replaced on the frame. It is used mainly for beginners and can be bought cheaply from most material stores.
(b) Silk: This is used mainly for hand printing and is stronger and finer than the above but does not have much stability.
(c) Nylon: This mesh is used widely as a general screen gauze. It is a mono-filament mesh, available in finer grades than the previous two, but not very stable and therefore should not be used for fine registration work.
(d) Polyester: This is a monofilament mesh which does not stretch with water and therefore is very good for all types of work. It is durable and strong and available in a large range of mesh sizes. It is especially good for very fine register work.

Mesh quality
'S', 'M', 'T' and 'H D' are varying thicknesses of meshes bought from screen printing suppliers – the 'S' types are woven with thin thread, 'M' medium, 'T' heavy and 'H D' extra heavy. The 'S' or 'M' types are used for general printing.

Stretching the mesh
Only cotton organdie or silk can effectively be stretched by hand. Although it is possible to stretch nylon over a frame, screen suppliers often do this better with automatic stretching devices.
(a) Stretching cotton organdie: The fabric should be cut to allow about 5 cm (2 in) extra around the whole area of the screen. It is important that the mesh is aligned correctly on the frame, with the warp and the weft threads running at 90° to each other and parallel to the sides of the frame. Begin in the middle of the two opposite sides. Pull the mesh tightly, following one particular thread between these two points, and fix with staples. Do this again on the opposite centre sides so that a cross of tension is formed. Continue pulling each opposite side in turn, working methodically outwards from the centre to the corner, until you have been all the way round the frame. Always staple around the sides of the frame, never on to the bottom, as this could make the base of the screen wobble. It is useful to staple into strips of card which eases the pulling out of the staples when the frame

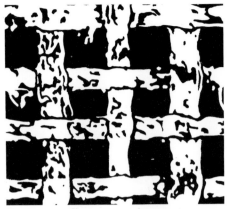

Cotton organdie.

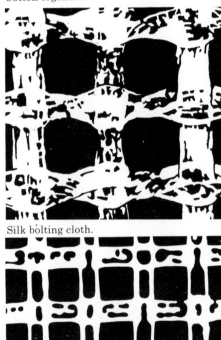

Silk bolting cloth.

Nylon monofilament.

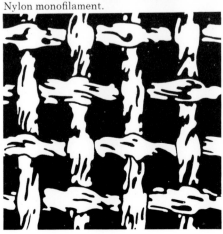

Polyester multifilament.

Left: *Steps and Ladders*
Handcut stencil screenprint 22″ × 30″
Patrick Hughes.

Above: *Crathes Castle Garden.*
Handpainted screenprint 30″ × 20″
Norman Stephens.

needs restretching. All the excess material is then cut away and the frame is ready for taping.

(b) Stretching silk mesh: Silk, made from the thread of a silkworm, has long been a screen fabric. It is often sold under the name of 'bolting cloth' because it was used by flour millers for sifting (bolting) bran from flour. The silk should be thoroughly moistened before stretching as this causes the threads to expand and become more elastic, so that when dry, maximum tension is obtained. The same method is used as in cotton organdie gradually allowing the pressure on the silk to build up.

(c) Stretching nylon, terylene and polyester: These fabrics are both elastic and extensible, the thinness and fineness of the mesh incorporating durability with resistance to abrasion. Nylon, termed 'monofilament', is a square weave material fused by heat at each intersection to keep its durability. Terylene has a further quality in that it absorbs much less water than nylon so that it retains its tautness even in the washing operation. For each particular mesh count manufacturers usually recommend the amount of stretch (about 4 per cent to 7 per cent), but it is difficult to pull a synthetic mesh drum tight by hand, and it is recommended that frames are stretched at screen printing suppliers on a machine.

Mesh preparation

After stretching a new mesh over a screen it is often necessary to wash it or treat it before a stencil can be used effectively on it. If organdie or silk mesh are being used, a wipe with warm water and detergent is sufficient. Nylon or terylene screens, which are very smooth when new, must be roughened a little to accept the stencil (given a 'key' or 'grip'). This is done either with a special degreasing agent purchased from specialist suppliers, or with caustic soda in a proportion of one part caustic soda to nine parts water. The solution is poured over the mesh and scrubbed for approximately ten minutes, and then rinsed off thoroughly with water or vinegar. The screen is then dried and is ready for the first stencil. One manufacturer recommends a scrub with warm water and scouring agent such as 'Vim'. This must only be done when the mesh is new as it will wear thin with constant use.

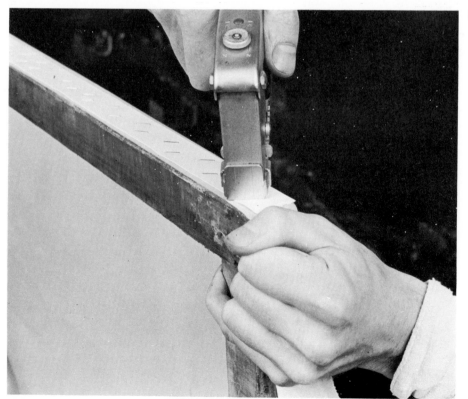

Stretching screen by hand.

Taping edges with gumstrip.

Taping

A well must be made for the ink to rest in the screen and a barrier must be made to prevent the ink from running under the frame whilst printing. This can be done with ordinary masking tape or at its best with brown tape. Brown tape will actually expand when wet so that on drying will pull the screen mesh tighter.

The tape is laid all the way around the inside of the screen frame and the first layer is folded at a right angle to the mesh and frame, half on the mesh, half on the frame. This prevents the ink seeping out under the sides. A second strip can be stuck overlapping the first. At the top end of the frame a third strip is stuck to form a well for the ink to rest in during printing.

Corner pieces are best pasted in to ensure no leakages at these points. On the back of the screen frame, a strip is pasted at the point where the mesh meets the frame to give added strength.

The brown tape is often renewed after each printing, although it is not necessary if oil based inks are being used, except after washing off a water based stencil. A coat of varnish over the top of the tape will preserve and protect it from water, and it will last through approximately five printings. If the screen has been used many times and the frame and tape are dirty it is advisable, if you wish to print a very pale colour or use white ink, to retape completely, covering also the frame sides and top with clean tape. This will ensure that the colour remains clean by preventing any old ink which has dried on the frame from mixing or discolouring whilst printing.

The squeegee

This is the tool used to force the ink through the screen mesh on to the paper below. It consists of a flexible, straight-edged blade sandwiched between two pieces of wood or metal which form the handle. The blade is usually made of rubber or plastic in the form of neoprene or polyurethane. It should be firm but pliable; the harder the blade the more pressure and energy is needed to make the stroke, and the thinner the deposit of printed ink.

The length of the squeegee depends on the size of the frame. It is useful to have several different sized squeegees for printing stencils of varying sizes, or more than one colour at a time. The largest may extend to within 5–8 cm (2–3 in) of the sides of the frame, whilst a tiny 10 cm (4 in) blade is useful for printing very small areas of colour.

Professional type squeegees with either wood or metal handles are supplied by most screen printing manufacturers and are measured by the centimetre. Blades are supplied either loose or in a handle. Polyurethane or plastic is recommended for its strength, durability and solvent resistance.

SCREEN PRINTING

Above: *Collected works.*
Silk-screen, autocut and photo-stencil
$24\frac{1}{2}'' \times 29''$
Jeffrey Edwards.

Right: *Lily Pond.*
Handpainted silk-screen $25'' \times 33\frac{1}{2}''$
Yvonne Cole.

94

SCREEN PRINTING

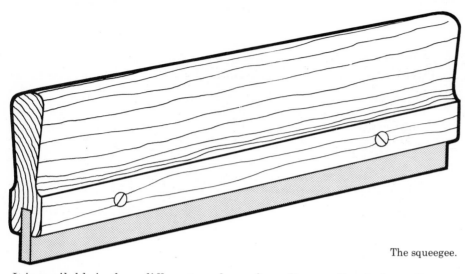

The squeegee.

It is available in three different grades: soft, medium and hard, depending on what type of work is being printed. Soft and medium are used for hand printing, hard for machine work. Rubber is not recommended for use on synthetic meshes, e.g. nylon, polyester and metal meshes. Most general screen printing suppliers will supply squeegees and separate blades for replacement.

A simple squeegee
Although a piece of varnished heavy card or floor tiling can be improvised for printing small areas, a simple squeegee up to 30·5 cm (12 in) in length is easily and quickly made from doorstop rubber, which is available from some hardware shops or specialist suppliers in the form of white or black natural rubber. This is simply glued or screwed into place between two lengths of wood with half of the rubber blade extending below the wood. A slightly longer strip of wood can be glued on the top to act as a handle.

Resharpening the blade
For clean, crisp printing the edges of the blade must always be kept sharp and square but after much wear they may become bent, warped or simply blunt. It is possible to trim a polyurethane blade using a wetted sharp knife and a steel rule, but this is not advisable when cutting off very small amounts. A more permanent squeegee sharpener consists of a piece of sand-paper stuck firmly down on to a board. This should be longer than the length of the squeegee. By evenly stroking the whole length of the blade over the sandpaper it can easily be resharpened at any time. A rounded blade is only preferred by fabric printers.

The beginners screen base
Having made a frame and a squeegee, a surface must be found or made on which to print. It is important that it is flat, very smooth and dust free. An area that is warped or has irregularities in its surface will be useless. The base must be larger than the screen area, and solid enough to stand a fair amount of pressure and remain perfectly rigid when being used. It need not necessarily be horizontal but can be tilted at an angle of 12° from back to front.

A formica topped table, hardboard or metal sheet can be used quite adequately but a portable baseboard that can be set up at any time is more convenient for a beginner and will allow printing to take place anywhere, even on the floor.

The frame can be attached to a base by a number of methods:
(a) By hinges screwed directly on to a baseboard top.
(b) By hinges screwed on to the baseboard sides.
(c) By separate hinge bar with coach bolts holding the screen in place.
(d) By a separate hinge bar attached underneath the baseboard to which the

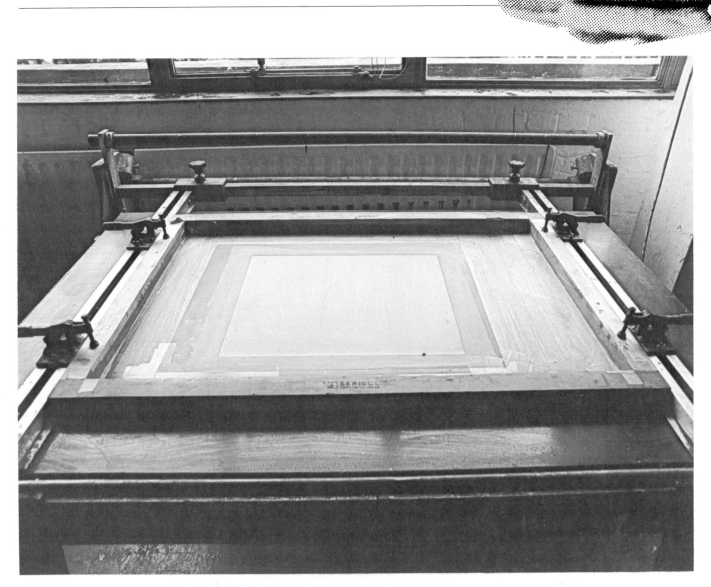

A vacuum bed screen printing table with taped-up screen ready for printing.

screen is attached with clamps.

A leg
This is a simple device which helps the screen to stand on its own when a print has been made, leaving two hands free to remove and rack the print. It consists simply of a strip of wood loosely screwed into the frame on the bottom left hand corner, and as the screen is lifted will automatically drop down to support the frame and keep it upright.

Vacuum printing tables
Screen printing tables with a vacuum baseboard and adjustable hinge gear on to which the frame fits are made in a variety of shapes and sizes. The base-board, drilled with small holes at 2·5 cm (1 in) intervals, is attached to a vacuum pump and this holds the paper in place when the screen is lowered, so making registration simpler. Small, cheaper hand-feed tables are produced by Peter Potter, Smith & Jones, Adelco, Hall-Mark and Register Print Machinery. They are the basic units normally used to print A1 size and not quite as stable as those produced by larger manufacturers.

Of the more expensive machines which incorporate durability, automatic vacuum operation, and micro-register apparatus (either by movement of bed or hinge gear), the 'Elite' tables produced by Marler combine a reliable table with good back-up servicing. Other manufacturers of popular tables include P.D.R. (Pronk Davies and Rusby), 'KPX' tables and Samco Strong 'Golia-Easy' tables (see p. 123).

SCREEN PRINTING

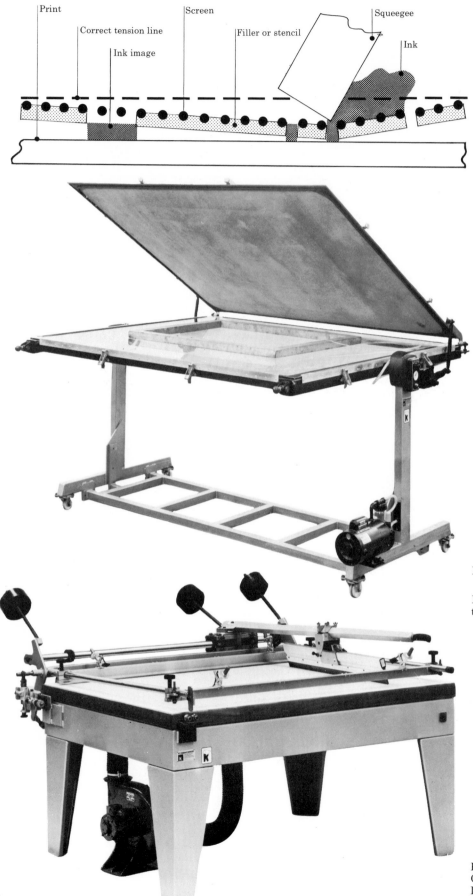

Print

Correct tension line

Ink image

Screen

Filler or stencil

Squeegee

Ink

The printing action of the squeegee forcing the ink through the open parts of the mesh. The squeegee should be held at an angle of approximately 45°.

Kipax vacuum printing down frame.

Kipax Quad Crown vacuum screen printing table.

Right: *Japan Gate 10*.
Open silk-screen 25″ × 18″
Liz Pannett.

46 TARUNA SERIES   Liz Pannett 1982

SCREEN PRINTING

STENCILS

In any screen print, it is the stencil that is used to make the image. There are many ways of making a stencil but in each method the actual stencil material acts as a block to the mesh and prevents the ink from printing on to the surface paper below: so that in all screen printing operations, the part of the mesh that is covered by a stencil remains in white on the printed image. When making a stencil for screen printing, it is therefore important to consider the work in negative. The stencil is generally attached to the underside of the mesh so that it cannot be dislodged by the action of the squeegee (on top).

In the screen printing process a separate stencil is required for each image but one stencil can be printed in a number of different colours. When selecting a stencil method, decisive factors are the quality of the image desired and the number of prints required. Each different method will produce different results and one stencil can be used for as little as five prints or as many as 500, depending on the toughness of the stencil material.

Handmade stencils

Although flat areas of colour can be printed through the screen without a stencil, brown tape does not produce a very precise edge. Different types of tape can be used for making stencils: sellotape and masking tape can all be used successfully with a little experimentation.

Lace doilies and computer tape are some of the simplest of stencils which, already cut, can simply be placed below the mesh and the action of the ink over the screen will hold them in place for a small number of printings.

Other simple stencils include 'Fablon', sticky labels of assorted shapes and sizes, and a typed impression can be obtained from using a Gestetner Roneo duplicating stencil.

Talcum powder, sprinkled on to the baseboard below, can be picked up and give a feathered effect for a small number of printings, and images from objects can be made by rubbing wax into the screen, which again will last for a small number of prints. This type of stencil making is termed 'direct' and is one in which a stencil is applied directly on to the mesh itself without an intermediary stage. Candlewax in its solid form is perhaps the easiest of wax based stencils and can be rubbed and drawn straight into the mesh itself.

Liquid screen stencils, often termed 'screen fillers' can also be applied directly to the mesh with a paintbrush. The type of filler required depends on the ink being used – the solvent (cleaner) of the ink must not dissolve the

Wax crayon on screen.

Adding filling.

Gumming screen with card.

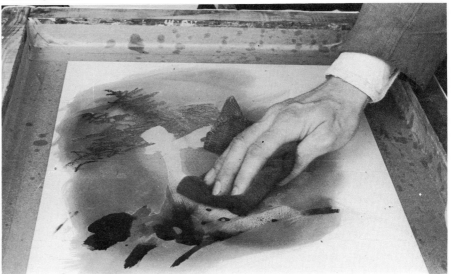

Washing out image with turps.

SCREEN PRINTING

screen filler. For example, if oil based inks are being used, a water based liquid should be used such as 'Le Page's' glue, fish glue or a specially manufactured filler (both fast and slow drying) marketed by specialist suppliers. If water based inks are being used, any oil based filler can be applied, e.g. oil paint, varnish, etc. and there are various other fillers that are not affected by either oil or water – such as shellac liquid, but this is almost impossible to remove from the screen. A cellulose filler is available from screen suppliers and is removed with its own appropriate cleaner and can be used with oil or water based inks.

The quality of the direct stencil made with a liquid is looser and gives more of a drawn quality, compared to the stencil which is cut with a knife.

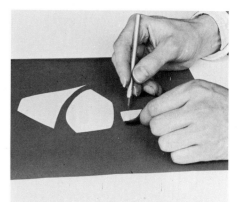

Cutting stencil.

Cut stencils

Cutting stencils by hand is one of the more traditional methods of screen printing in which a hard edge to the printed colour is obtained. Paper is one of the simplest, basic forms of cut stencil and is readily available, easy to use and has infinite possibilities. An advantage of using newsheet (or tracing paper) is that the action of the ink over the screen is enough to hold it in place for a long run. Simple or complex shapes can be cut from a newsheet with a very sharp knife. If there are large 'floating' areas or loose parts in the stencil, they will attach themselves to the screen if placed in the correct position on the baseboard.

Hand cut film

Many designs require more complicated cutting than can be achieved with any of the previous stencils. Others involve large runs and a cleaning operation in the middle of printing to change colours. In these cases special films are available which enable the cutter to control intricate detail and fine line registration and to clean up and leave the stencil intact. These films are marketed only by specialist suppliers and each brand has its own particular application to the mesh. Each one sheet of film is composed of two layers of material held together with a temporary glue – a transparent backing sheet, often plastic, and on top a very thin stencil material. Each type is tinted a different colour and is generally semi-transparent to allow tracing and direct cutting.

Attaching stencil to screen.

The stencil film should always be cut about 7·5 cm (3 in) larger than the area required to print. The parts required to print should be cut out on a hard surface using a very sharp knife. Only careful pressure is exerted on the knife so that it does not cut through the transparent backing sheet and the pieces that have been cut out are peeled off and thrown away.

Spreading blue filler.

Colour printing

Where colours are required to meet each other without a white line separating them, each separate colour stencil must be cut to overlap the previous print edges by a fraction of a centimetre ($\frac{1}{8}$ in) printing the lightest colour first and darkest last. If a print of more than two colours is being made, it is advisable after printing the first colour to cut the second stencil from that first printing and so on, i.e. not to cut six stencils all at once from the original design. Some movement of the stencil may occur whilst printing, and the only way to combat this is to cut each stencil from the preceding colour print.

Types of hand cut film stencils

Depending on what type of ink you are using to print with, i.e. water based or oil based, a stencil should be chosen that is the opposite base to the ink.
(a) Profilm (Stenplex Amber): This is an amber-coloured, shellac-based film and can be used with either water or oil based inks, and is the cheapest of specially prepared cut film stencils. It should not be attached to man-made fibres, such as nylon or terylene, as the mesh is liable to damage with heat. It can easily be attached to and removed from various meshes by following the maker's instructions.

Peeling off filler.

(b) Autocut: There are many differing kinds of water-based stencil films on the market and of the most recent is 'Autocut'. It is a pink tinted film, easily cut, with mistakes able to be re-laid, and is quickly attached to and removed from the screen by following the simple maker's instructions.

Photographic stencils

Making a photographic stencil necessitates a little more time and effort than a handmade stencil. The photo-stencil itself is made in a contact frame in which there is a sandwich of a photographic positive and either the photo-stencil material or a sensitised liquid which has been applied and dried directly onto the screen itself.

The contact frame is generally sited in a darkroom where most of the work is prepared. During the exposure, the film and positive must come into contact with a very bright light source after which the stencil is developed and dried on the screen ready for printing.

Making the positive

A positive is made on to a piece of transparent film. It contains areas which are light proof and areas which will allow the light to pass through. The image area itself must be light proof (i.e. black) and can be made in a variety of ways: it can be drawn directly (with photo-opaque, indian ink, Letraset, oil crayon) on to a film (which can be clear acetate or a polyester drafting film) or it can be produced photographically on to a sheet of film. It must be stressed that in all cases the positive must consist of areas of black and clear and that the image required to print must be the black (i.e. light proof) areas. Photographic stencils cannot reproduce any tone or grey areas – these are produced by an illusion of 'half tone' dots in black and clear to give the impression of grey tones.

Types of photographic stencils

(a) Direct photo-stencils: These are in liquid form and an advantage, apart from their cheapness, is their durability and ability to produce very fine quality detail. It is best when making these stencils to use a coloured mesh to prevent any under-cutting by light reflection. The stencils can be made on a variety of meshes and the screen coating should be carried out normally in a darkroom and dried in total darkness. Examples of these liquid stencils are

Coating screen with photo-emulsion.

Washing off emulsion.

'Seriset B' (Sericol, see p. 123) and 'Seriset S' (Sericol), the latter for use where very strong solvents are being used.

There is a large range of stencil emulsions on the market and it is important to choose the correct stencil material to suit your mesh and inks, and to follow the maker's instructions very carefully when processing the emulsions. It is normal to use a coating trough but a piece of card or plastic can be used to pull the liquid over the screen.

(b) Indirect photo-stencils: The advantage of indirect stencils is the rendering of very fine details in halftones and line images and maximum sharpness in contours. Indirect stencils consist of a film carrier (paper, plastic or polyester) coated on one side with a light-sensitive pigmented gelatine. They can be purchased either already sensitised or in an unsensitised form.

Examples of presensitised stencils are: 'Autostar' (Sericol), a turquoise-coloured stencil which needs no hardening and after exposure is washed out with cold water in normal light. Some difficulty may be found in removal from the mesh unless a stencil remover is used or a high pressure washing gun. Also in a similar category are: 'Colorgraph Gamma' from P.D.R. and 'Waterfix' from Marler. 'Five star' from Sericol is a stencil which should be exposed dry and processed in subdued light, developed in hydrogen peroxide and washed out with warm water at 43°C/110°F. Similar films are made by other suppliers.

An example of an unsensitised stencil is 'Sericol Red' which is a photo-stencil material coated on to paper, sensitised in a bichromate solution and exposed when wet.

Light sources

In general, photographic screen printing stencils are sensitive to ultra violet light. The close contact of the positive with the photographic film (or coated

screen) must be placed in front of this light source for a certain length of time, which can vary from half a minute to thirty minutes.

To do this in the screen printing trade, especially made light boxes, called 'printing down frames', have been manufactured. They have very tight fitting vacuum operated lids to keep the contact of film and positive whilst exposure takes place. It is not always necessary to use such a powerful light source, various others, such as mercury vapour and metal halogen, can be used and experimentation must take place to find the right light source and exposure to suit your pocket and your operation.

For the beginner, a vacuum bag of 'copysac' can be used with a light source suspended above it. These sacs are made from clear plastic and are attached to a vacuum motor which keeps the esential contact of positive and film whilst exposure takes place.

Even simpler devices can be worked out at home with a little ingenuity – a sheet of glass placed over the contact with weights on top might be sufficient for a beginner.

Graphoscreen exposure unit, also designed for use with photo-lithography and photo-etching.

Degreasing screens and stencil adhesion
Before attempting to apply any photographic stencil to the screen mesh either directly or indirectly, the mesh must be thoroughly degreased or it will reject the stencil. 'Fairy Liquid', French chalk and 'Vim' have been used in the past to remove the grease from the mesh but it is most common more recently to purchase the relevant degreaser from a specialist supplier.

INKS, REGISTRATION & PRINTING

Inks
Like other methods of printing, the screen technique requires its own special type of ink. This basically consists of a finely ground pigment suspended in a base. The base is generally the reverse of the ingredient of the stencil, i.e. when printing with oil based inks, a stencil that is water soluble is used so that the inks do not interfere with the stencil in any way.

An important feature of screen inks is their consistency. The right consistency stops the ink from running through the mesh directly it is poured on to the screen, and yet allows the squeegee blade to flow smoothly over the screen during printing. Only constant testing and experience will allow the screen printer to become thoroughly conversant with the process, but the following may act as a guide: the correct consistency of oil based inks can be likened to thin cream and that of water based inks to thick cream, allowing a thin layer of colour to be printed in each case.

Only a little ink is deposited each time a print is made, but a larger amount of ink is kept in the screen so that at least ten prints can be made before the supply needs replenishing. Each colour must be allowed to dry thoroughly before any overprinting begins.

Water based inks
These inks are used very little in the trade today except perhaps for fabric printing. The advantages that they have for beginners are that they are cheap, easy to make or improvise and do not require specialist thinners or cleaning liquids. A binder for the pigment can be something as simple as wallpaper paste or a solution of gum arabic crystals and water, or can be bought as such direct from a specialist supplier. Any finely ground colour pigment can be added to the base – poster paint, 'Dylon' dyes, or pigments such as 'Analine' dyes or 'Polyprint' colour among others.

Oil based inks
These are available generally only from specialist suppliers who will send a catalogue and price list on request. They are made by adding pigment to a base of either synthetic resin or boiled linseed oil and there is a wide variety

SCREEN PRINTING

Another repeat.
Silk-screen 20″ × 30″
Mike Robbins.

American dream.
Silk-screen, collage 20″ × 25″
Allan Bamford.

SCREEN PRINTING

Various solvents and fillers used in the silk-screen workshop.

of finishes to include matt, silk and gloss effects, which can be bought as strong, often brilliant, opaque colour, the range including silver, gold and fluorescent inks. A huge range of inks are made by specialist manufacturers for every conceivable application: glass, perspex, plastics, metals. These are usually either plastic or cellulose-based, and unfortunately need their own special thinners and cleaners which are expensive and often produce unpleasant smells. When you have chosen a manufacturer whose range of inks you prefer, it is best to keep to that particular range as not all types of oil-bound inks mix together.

Mixing

Water based inks are best mixed in glass jars or waxed or plastic cups and should be stored with lids on.

Oil based inks can be mixed in tin cans, jars, but not in plastic or polystyrene containers as they will eventually melt them. Ink straight out of the can is too thick to use directly and should be thinned, generally with white spirit, from between 10 per cent to 33 per cent until the correct consistency is achieved. If colours are to be mixed together (e.g. blue and yellow) it should be done before thinning.

A transparent colour can be made by adding a small part of the colour to its base. When using opaque oil based inks, a special base called 'reducing' or 'extender' base must be used. The colour must always be added to the base and in very small amounts, then dabbed out on a sheet of paper to test its transparency.

It is important to make a test of each mixed colour on paper and let it dry so that you know exactly what colour you have mixed before beginning to print. Dried ink is not always the same colour as when wet in the pot.

Most varieties of ink are quick drying and will dry within half an hour to an hour of printing so that several colours can be be printed on the same day.

Registration

It is important to be able to choose where the image is to be printed on the paper. Various methods of registration exist, also allowing correct placing of many colours within a printed image. The printed image must remain in the same position on each printing sheet throughout the 'run' or 'edition' (total number of prints made) so that accurate placing of the next colour may follow. If the screen is firmly hinged to the printing base, half the problem is solved.

A master drawing or a simple, accurate plan of the printed image must be made on to cartridge paper to facilitate the placing of the registration marks.

The easiest method is to use a clear acetate piece of film that is large enough to cover the whole of the printing paper. This is attached to the base down the left hand side and a single print taken. The acetate can then be lifted up and the master drawing or first colour print is placed on the base and the printed acetate then flipped back on top. Because the acetate is clear

it is possible to move the print or drawing into whatever position is necessary, make registration marks and then remove the acetate altogether.

Registration marks are neatly termed 'lays' or 'stops' and are made by placing masking tape (or bits of card) along two edges and the corner between the two sides. They are cut approximately 5 cm (2 in) long and taped to the baseboard and remain in position whilst the print run is made. Each time a new print is made it is slid carefully, gently and exactly into these lays. Care should be taken to ensure that the paper does not slip underneath the masking tape or card stops as this will cause misregistration.

Each time a new stencil is put on the screen, new registration marks must be made. The second colour can be registered in the same way as the first, providing its position has been marked on a first colour print or on the master drawing.

The acetate is usually taken away once the lays have been positioned and can be cleaned and re-used; but if mistakes or white gaps between the colours are increasing as the edition is being printed, the acetate flap can be used to register each print individually provided it has been left in its original position.

Printing

A print is made by pulling the ink, with a squeegee, from the top of the screen, over the mesh and stencil, to the bottom of the frame. Each pull of the squeegee, from top to bottom, results in one print on to the paper beneath. The print is taken away to dry and another sheet of paper is fed into the lays and the action repeated.

Although the action of pulling is one of the most important techniques, all the skill required can be obtained with a little practice and observation, and compared to the screen preparation which initially takes a long time, the printing process itself is a very fast one. Once you have achieved a rhythm, over fifty prints can be taken in an hour.

It is most important to be well organised and have inks, paper, rags, cleaning fluid ready beforehand. It may be necessary to rub in a barrier cream as inks may be harsh on hands. A small amount of ink should be mixed up if this is the first attempt at printing, approximately 0.28 litre ($\frac{1}{2}$ pint) of ink will print anything from ten to fifty prints. A stencil will take six or seven pulls to settle down, so an amount of old paper is needed to 'proof' or practice on to before the edition is made. Roughly 2–3 per cent of spoilage is estimated for an experienced printer, and for a beginner, much more!

Before printing begins it is necessary to set up the frame and bed ready for editioning. The actual screen frame and mesh are lifted above the printing base (be it a table or a special vacuum printing bed) by approximately $\frac{1}{10}-\frac{1}{4}$ in (3–7 mm) by taping small pieces of card $\frac{1}{2}$ in (12 mm) in size to the underside of the screen frame, or by heightening the adjustable hinge gear at the back of a vacuum printing table. This is termed the 'snap off' gap and will help the image to remain sharp during printing and will hopefully prevent the paper from sticking to the screen during printing operations.

Printing method

(a) After having chosen a squeegee that overlaps the stencil each side by at least 2·5 cm (1 in), the paper is placed in position. The screen is lowered on to the base and the ink is poured evenly into the well at the top of the frame. The squeegee is gripped firmly with both hands, one at each end, fingers spreading along the edge of the wood. This will exert the pressure necessary to make the print. The ink is collected with the front edge of the blade of the squeegee.

(b) It is important to keep the blade at an angle of approximately 45° when making the stroke. Collect all the ink and pull the squeegee and ink with a firm even pressure, over the whole area of the screen in one direction (generally towards yourself) from the top to bottom of the frame. The squeegee action must be consistent in one direction; a pull in any other direction

SCREEN PRINTING

1. Registering paper with sticky tape.

2. Pouring on ink asphaltum.

3. Printing first colour.

4. Acetate overlay to register.

5. Registering first print under acetate.

6. New registration for second print.

7. Printing second colour.

8. Finished print.

may shift the stencil and alter the image position.

(c) At the end of the stroke, the screen frame is lifted slightly and either the ink is scooped up on to the edge of the squeegee blade and deposited back at the top of the frame in the well, or it is pushed back gently over the mesh and returned to the well leaving the stencil covered with a layer of ink. This is called a 'flood stroke' and is the method practised by most professional screen printers as it acts to prevent the screen from drying up whilst using thin film screen inks. Different meshes need different techniques and experimentation will help you to decide which method to use.

(d) The squeegee is left in the top of the frame with the ink and the frame is propped (or hinged) up waiting for the next sheet of paper.

(e) Once a rhythm has begun, it is wise not to hesitate but to keep printing steadily as any interruption will cause no end of problems – e.g. ink drying in the stencil therefore image not printing well.

(f) In multi-colour work, when the edition has been completed and is hung up to dry, the screen is cleaned and the stencil removed ready for the next stencil to be put on. Registration takes place exactly as before and each subsequent colour is printed in a separate printing.

(g) It is generally true that each colour requires a separate printing but two or even three colours can be printed in the screen at the same time. The areas required should be partitioned off separately and using small squeegees, one colour is printed directly after the other without lifting the screen; the result being two or three colours printing simultaneously on different parts of the print.

(h) Each wet print is then hung or laid to dry after each pull of the squeegee. Racking systems for storing wet prints until they are dry can vary from a set of clothes pegs strung on a washing line to a sophisticated hinged metal tray rack. The latter is probably preferable if your pocket will allow as it is built for the screen printer interested in producing quantities of prints. Each rack allows the prints to dry horizontally on a metal grid which is hinged with a spring to allow the trays to easily be lifted or lowered as the need arises.

CLEANING UP

Finally, the cleaning operation is quite straightforward but can be messy unless a certain amount of care is taken. An apron or some type of protective clothing should be worn and plenty of rags, old newspapers and a bin should be kept handy. The excess ink is scraped out of the frame and replaced in the ink pot.

The squeegee is cleaned first as the blade can be damaged easily by trying to scrape off dried ink. Newspapers are placed under the screen mesh and the frame lowered on top. The mesh should be flooded with whatever solvent is necessary and the excess ink loosened and mopped up with old cloths (strong paper towel can be used). This operation is repeated until most of the ink is removed. A clean cloth is then used to take away the final traces of ink, making sure that the brown tape area, including the sides, are especially clean. If small areas are proving difficult, two small cloths rubbed simultaneously on either side will absorb the rest. There will be some staining of the mesh by the colour of the ink but this must not be confused with a blocked screen. If the screen is blocked the crossed mesh threads will not be seen clearly when the screen is held up to the light. For stubborn blocks of dried ink, strong cleaners are available in liquid or spray form from specialist suppliers.

If the stencil has remained on the screen, the appropriate dissolving agent should now be used to remove it. It is possible, if the stencil is to be used again, to leave it on once the mesh has been cleaned.

Frame, base and squeegee should then be left immaculately clean, ready for the next printing session.

APPENDIX:

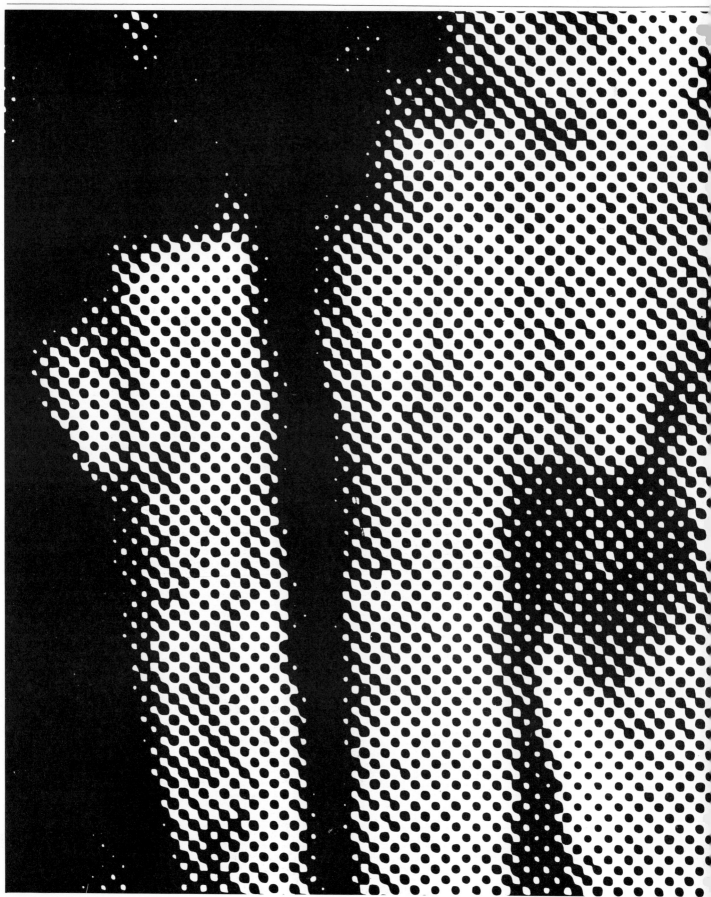

PROCESS PHOTOGRAPHY

APPENDIX: PROCESS PHOTOGRAPHY

IN ORDER TO MAKE prints from a photograph or piece of artwork, the tonal gradations of the original must be converted into a combination of opaque and transparent areas. When reproduced on film, the new version of the image can be transferred to lithographic or etched plates or a silk-screen by the use of light-sensitive coatings which harden on exposure to light, allowing the unexposed areas to be washed away by a solvent. The prime requirements for process photography, by which the transformation from original image to one suitable for reproduction is effected, are methodical working practice and careful observation: given these, the various procedures allow considerable versatility in reproduction.

Transformation of the image is carried out using either a process camera, in which light is directed onto the original and reflected through the lens, or a darkroom enlarger, in which the light is transmitted through a continuous tone negative. In both cases, special lith film is used.

Lith films may have a base of paper, acetate or polyester. The first type, generally known as document papers, are designed for contact printing from books or documents, and while they are relatively cheap, they suffer from the drawbacks of dimensional instability, lack of sensitivity to fine detail and a tendency to blur the image by veiling on the edges of the black areas. Stronger and thicker bases give improved dimensional stability, acetate being stable enough for most applications, while polyester bases are strong enough to allow the backing to be made thin enough to allow the exposure to be made through the base, giving a laterally reversed image where this is required. A typical film base will be five or six thousandths of an inch (0·13 or 0·15 mm) thick, maximum thickness being eight thou (0·20 mm) and minimum thickness, for exposure through the base, being four thou (0·10 mm) polyester or three thou (0·80 mm) acetate.

The special lith emulsion used on the films is composed of fine-grain halide with a high silver content to give very high contrast and slow working speeds, and the coating is very thin for maximum sharpness of definition. Although the slowest document papers may be used in low-level artificial light, and others may be non-colour sensitive, and able to be used in yellow safelight, standard lith films are orthographic, or sensitive only to blue-green light, and must be used with a red safelight, while panchromatic films, used for colour separations and sensitive to all colours, are restricted to total darkness. Two further types of lith film are direct-positive and ready screened. The former has a very high-contrast emulsion which produces a positive image by contact printing from a positive original, and can be handled in artificial light; the latter is used for making half-tones without the use of a half-tone screen, and requires red safelight.

In developing lith film, a special developer based on a formaldehyde-quinone formula is used. This works on the principle of 'infectious development', starting very slowly and building up the image with increasing speed as a result of the formation of semi-quinone developing agents during the process.

Because of the infectious nature of the development great care must be exercised during the final stages, as the process gathers speed, to avoid over-development and image spread within the emulsion itself, though the thinness of the lith emulsion helps to retard image spread. Moreover, the effectiveness of lith developer is greatly reduced at temperatures below 10°C (50°F), so that working temperature needs to be monitored, and the developer itself deteriorates quickly when stored. Ideally, fresh developer should be used for each piece of film.

For the most detailed work, still bath development is best: after a few seconds of agitation at the start to ensure the film is thoroughly wetted, the developing bath is left still. The resulting formation of stale developer on the surface of the film helps inhibit development, particularly at the edges of the black areas, thus avoiding bleeding of those areas and blurring of fine detail.

The more normal method of development is by agitation. To give even development of the image, the bath is tilted towards each side in turn for two minutes, washing the emulsion evenly in developer, then left still until the

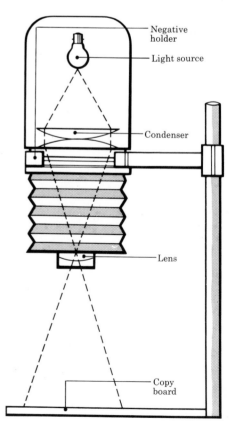

The enlarger.

Negative holder

Light source

Condenser

Lens

Copy board

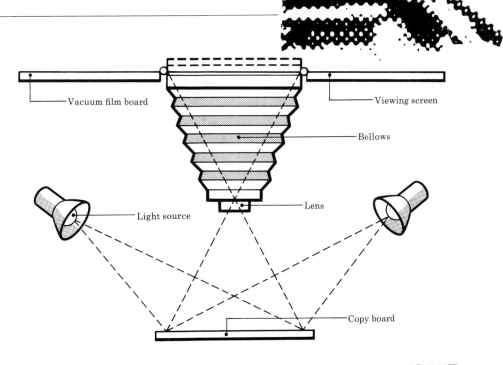

The process camera.

Labels on diagram: Vacuum film board, Viewing screen, Bellows, Light source, Lens, Copy board

required density is achieved. Generally, two to three minutes at 20°C (68°F) will prove adequate for full development, with the slower still bath requiring slightly longer than the agitation method. In either case, with the speed increasing towards the end of the process, the film should be watched closely until development is judged to be complete: safelighting is essential, and the ideal arrangement is a safelight set into the bench, used in conjunction with a transparent dish.

The film image from which the plates are to be made will need to be positive or negative, right-reading or wrong-reading (laterally reversed), according to the nature of the final printing process, as it is vital to keep the emulsion of the film in contact with the plate or stencil to avoid distortion of the image. For silk-screen and photo-engraving intaglio work, a right-reading positive is required; relief photo-engraving calls for a right-reading negative; and for lithography the positive or negative image, depending on the method of working, will need to be right-reading for direct and wrong-reading for offset printing: in all these cases, the image is referred to as it appears when viewed from the emulsion side. Where a laterally reversed image is required, the film in the process camera should be exposed through the base, and special film is available without the anti-halation layer present in normal film which will impair definition of base exposures.

LINE IMAGES

A line image is composed of areas of solid black, making it particularly suitable for the reproduction of black and white originals and high-contrast photographs. At the same time, while much of the detail in a continuous tone photograph will be lost in the reproduction, the line image can give an adequate representation, as well as lending itself to a variety of special effects. Whatever the final results aimed at, the first step is to make test strips to establish the appropriate ratio of aperture to exposure, progressively doubling the exposure time and masking the areas already exposed with black paper. The strip can then be developed and the desired exposure selected.

An alternative method, where line positives are required, is to use the enlarger to make positives direct from an original negative. Depending on whether a right-reading or wrong-reading image is required, the emulsion of the negative should face, respectively, away from or towards the enlarger light and lith film instead of photographic paper is used to receive the image:

150 line screen conversion.

120 line screen conversion.

line screen conversion.

Line conversion.

again, a test strip should be made first. The image received by the film will be an enlarged version of the normally indistinguishable clusters of silver grains in the negative emulsion.

HALFTONE IMAGES

Whereas the line process can reproduce a considerable amount of detail, it can convey little subtlety as far as tonal gradations are concerned, and in order to reproduce these the image must be broken up into a more regular pattern than the randomly dispersed shapes of the line copy. To achieve this regularity a halftone screen is used to impose a regular grid through which the original is photographed. Variations in the size of dots produced in this way will give the illusion of continuous tones.

The original form of halftone screen was a finely ruled glass screen, placed close to the emulsion of the film in the process camera. This allowed full illumination of the film by the light reflected from the original at the centre of each of the apertures of the grid, and, being effectively out of focus as far as the image was concerned, the resulting dots gradually tapered to almost nothing directly behind the rules of the grid, the size of the resulting dots varying according to the amount of light reflected by any given area of the image.

The glass screen, which needed to be positioned at a critical distance from the film, has been superseded by the contact screen, which is a film covered with a regular pattern of vignetted dots, and which can be used either in a process camera or in an enlarger. Various rulings of screen are available, the coarsest screens giving the greatest contrast but with a consequent degradation of tonal quality.

It is important to match the screen to the paper on which the prints will be made. Screens with rulings as low as 45 lines per inch (18 lines per centimetre) and as high as 225 lines/in (89 lines/cm) are available, the former being suitable for the coarsest papers, such as low-grade newsprint, while the latter requires the highest quality chromo paper and is impractical for normal use. The most widely used screens are in the range of 60–150 lines/in (24–59 lines/cm), with 120 lines/in (47 lines/cm) being adequate for most purposes. Screens are also available with irregular dot formations, and varied effects can be obtained by using the mesh patterns of open-weave fabrics held between sheets of glass to make improvised screens.

It is also necessary to keep the minimum and maximum size of dot within the limits which the different printing media can reproduce satisfactorily. The size of dot is expressed as the percentage of black present in the dot, as illustrated by the accompanying halftone percentage scale. In a halftone positive, the highlights will have only a very small dot, described as 5 per cent, and in the darkest areas the black will be as high as 95 per cent; a halftone negative, naturally, will reverse the scale, so that the highlights appear as 95 per cent black and the shadows as 5 per cent. The chart gives guidelines for the appropriate percentages of black at either end of the tonal scale for the various printing processes.

Contact screens should be used with a vacuum baseboard and should overlap the film for perfect contact, and normally the emulsion of the screen should be in contact with the emulsion of the film. However, where a right-reading negative or wrong-reading positive is required for platemaking, as dictated by the final printing process, the exposure should be made through the base of the film, in which case the screen will be placed against the base rather than the emulsion.

Using the process camera to make a halftone negative, an initial flash exposure is made, using a low-level light source positioned some 4 ft (1·2 m) from the film, to establish the image of the screen and sensitise the emulsion so that the dots in the dark areas of the image can be formed at the same time as the mid-tone and highlight dots: unless the inertia of the film is overcome

by the flash exposure the light reflected by the dark areas will be insufficient to form a dot by the time the lighter areas are fully exposed. The main exposure which follows establishes the image on the film as a regular pattern of dots of various sizes. The ratio of the two exposures governs both the size of dot found at the extremes of the tonal scale and the overall contrast of the image.

To make a halftone positive from a continuous tone negative, the enlarger is used. Again, the emulsion of the screen should be in contact with the emulsion of the lith film, overlapping the film and held in place by a vacuum board, or by a weighted sheet of glass where no vacuum board is available. The negative should be placed with the emulsion facing away from or towards the light source according to whether a right-reading or wrong-reading positive is required. As with the process camera, a flash exposure is required to register the screen image, followed by the main exposure to register the image, though the exposure times will normally be shorter using the transmitted light of the enlarger than with the reflected light of the process camera.

Similar procedures are followed when working with ready-screened emulsions, except that the contact screen is omitted.

PROCESS PHOTOGRAPHY

Process	Film image	Tonal Scale		
	Looking at emulsion	Highlight	Shadow	
Silk-screen	Right-reading positive	10%	95%	Both highlight and shadow dots are reduced in size in contacting and platemaking, so that the very small dots produced by fine halftone screens may pass between the threads of the silk-screen mesh. To prevent this, the halftone screen used must have no more than half the number of lines per inch as the silk-screen mesh has threads per inch.
Photo-engraving Letterpress or relief	Right-reading negative	75%	5%	Although the halftone negative has a restricted tonal range, the action of the acid during the etching process will reduce the size of the highlight dots, which have the longest exposure to the acid. Consequently, these must be made larger in the negative to avoid being completely eroded by the action of the acid; after etching, they will be reduced to the correct 90–95 per cent.
Intaglio	Right-reading positive	0–5%	90%	Leaving the lightest areas of the positive transparency completely free of dots will result in the surface of the plate being completely smooth in those areas after the transference of the image, thus giving extra brilliance in the white areas of the print. During contacting, the shadow dots will be reduced in size, and it is important to keep a regular shadow dot in the darker areas to avoid them being etched flat by the acid, which will result in the shadows being no more than light grey in the finished print.
Lithography Direct, neg working	Right-reading negative	98%	10%	Clear white highlights and solid blacks in the darkest areas should be the aim. Because of the tendency of the ink to fill in the smallest shadow dots in the printing process, these should be slightly larger for direct than for offset lithography.
Direct, pos working	Right-reading positive	2%	90%	
Offset, neg working	Wrong-reading negative	100–98%	5%	
Offset, pos working	Wrong-reading positive	0–2%	95%	

BIBLIOGRAPHY

Screen Printing
Auvil, Kenneth W. *Serigraphy: Silk Screen Techniques for the Artist* New Jersey: Prentice-Hall 1965

Baker, F. A. *Silk Screen Practice* London: Blandford Press 1934

Biegeleisen, J. I. *The Complete Book of Silk Screen Printing Production* New York: Dover Publications 1963

Biegeleisen, J. I. and **Cohen M. A**. *Silk Screen Techniques* New York: Dover Publications 1958

Carr, Francis *A Guide to Screen Process Printing* London: Studio Vista 1961

Hiett, Harry L., edited by H. K. Middleton *Silk Screen Process Production* London: Blandford Press 1950, 1960

Kinsey, Anthony *Introducing Screen Printing* London: Batsford 1967; New York: Watson-Guptill 1968

Kosloff, Albert *The Art and Craft of Screen Process Printing* New York: The Bruce Publishing Co. 1960

Mara, T. *Screenprinting*. Thames & Hudson 1979

Middleton, H. K. *Silk Screen Process: A Volume of Technical References* London: Blandford Press 1949

Russ, Stephen *Practical Screen Printing* London: Studio Vista 1969; New York; Watson-Guptill 1969

Turner, Silvie *Basic Screenprint* Batsford 1975

Shokler, Harry *Artists Manual for Silk Screen Print Making* New York: American Artists Group 1946

Withers, Gerald (editor) *Screen Printing Point of Sale and Industries Manual* London: Batiste Publications 1967

Wolfe, Herbert J. *Printing and Litho Inks* New York; MacNair-Dorland Company 1957

Lithography
Antreasian, Garo Z. and **Adams, Clinton** *The Tamarind Book of Lithography: Art and Techniques* New York: Tamarind Lithography Workshop Inc. and Harry N. Abrams Inc. 1971

Cliffe, H. *Lithography* London: Studio Vista 1965

Jones, Stanley *Lithography for Artists* London: Oxford University Press 1967

Knigin, Michael and **Zimiles, Murray** *The Technique of Fine Art Lithography* New York: Van Nostrand Reinhold 1970

Trivick, H. *Autolithography* London: Faber and Faber 1960

Vicary, Richard, *The Thames and Hudson Manual of Lithography* London: Thames and Hudson 1976

Senefelder, Alors, *A Complete Course in Lithography* New York: Da Capo Press 1968

Relief Printing
Erikson, J. and **Sproul, A**., *Relief Printing Without a Press* London: Van Nostrand Reinhold 1979

Green, Peter *Creative Print Making* London: Batsford 1964

Green, peter *Introducing Surface Printing* London: Batsford 1967

O'Connor, J. *Introducing Relief Printing* London: Batsford

O'Connor, J. *Relief Printing* London: Batsford

O'Connor, J. *Technique of Wood Engraving* London: Batsford 1970

Ross, J. and **C. Romano** *The Complete Relief Print* London: Collier-Macmillan 1974

Rothenstein, Michael *Frontiers of Printmaking* London: Studio Vista 1962

Rothenstein, Michael *Linocuts and Woodcuts* London: Studio Vista 1962; New York: Watson-Guptill 1964

Rothenstein, Michael *Relief Printing* London: Studio Vista 1970; New York: Watson-Guptill 1970

Etching, Engraving and Process Photography
Ammonds, C. C. *Photoengraving: Principles and Practice* London: Pitman 1966

Buckland-Wright, J. *Etching* London: Studio Publications 1953

Cartwright, H. M. *Ilford Graphic Arts Manual* Vol. I London: Ilford 1961

Chamberlain, W. *Manual of Etching and Engraving* London: Thames and Hudson 1973; New York: Viking Press 1973

Chambers, Eric *Camera and Process Work* London: Ernest Benn 1964

Griffiths, A. *Prints and Printmaking* London: British Museum Publications 1980

Gross, Anthony *Etching, Engraving and Intaglio Printing* London: Oxford University Press 1970

Hamerton, P. H. *Etching and Etchers* New York: Macmillan 1976

Lumsden, E. S. *The Art of Etching* London: Constable 1963; New York: Dover 1963

Pateman, F. and **Young, L. C.** *Printing Science* London: Pitman 1969

Tyrrell, A. *Basics of Reprography* London: Focal Press; New York: Hastings 1972

General

Brunner, Felix *A Handbook of Graphic Reproduction Processes* London: Alec Tiranti 1962

Daniels, Harvey *Printmaking* London: Hamlyn 1971

Gilman, Pat *Modern Prints* London: Studio Vista 1970

Gilman, Pat *Understanding Prints* London: Waddington Gallery

Heller, J. *Printmaking Today* New York: Holt, Rinehart and Winston 1972

Peterdi, Gabor *Printmaking* London: Collier Macmillan 1970

Peterdi, Gabor *Printmaking* New York: Macmillan 1959

Salamon, F. *Collector's Guide to Prints and Printmakers* London: Thames and Hudson 1972

Turner, S. *Handbook of Printmaking Supplies* London: Printmakers Council 1978

EUROPEAN SUPPLIERS

Adana (Printing Machines) Ltd, 15-19 Church Street, Twickenham, Middlesex. London Showrooms, 8 Grays Inn Road, WC1 (*Small printing machines and associated equipment*)

Adelco Screen Process Ltd., Weydon Lane, Farnham, Surrey (*Process cameras*)

Agfa-Gevaert Ltd, 20 Piccadilly, London W1 (*Photographic equipment*)

Allied Industrial Services, Duncombe Road, Bradford, Yorkshire BD7 2QS (*Cleaning cloths and dust control*)

Atlantis Paper Co. F3 Warehouse, Garnet Street, London E1 (*Fine papers and general supplies*)

Ault & Wiborg Ltd, 71 Standen Road, London SW18 (*Printing ink and rollers*)

Autotype Co. Ltd., Brownlow Road, London W13 (*Stencil films*)

Berrick Bros Ltd, 142 Vauxhall Street, London SE11 (*Paper*)

Blackwell & Co. Ltd, Sugar House Lane, Stratford, London E15 2QN (*Screen printing ink*)

A. G. W. Britton & Sons Ltd, 27 Willow Way, London SE26 (*Screen printing ink*)

Buck & Ryan, 101 Tottenham Court Road, London W1P 0DY (*Etching and engraving tools*)

Burleighfield Printing Studios, High Wycombe, Buckinghamshire (*Fine art editioning services and instruction in direct and offset lithography, intaglio, screen printing, and photo-mechanical work*)

R. K. Burt & Co. Ltd, 37 Union Street, London SE1 1SD (*Hand-made and mould-made papers*)

Cartiere Enrico Magnani S.P.A., Piazza Matteotti No. 11, 51017 Pescia (Pistoya), Italy (*Paper*)

F. Charbonnel, 13 Quai Montebello, Paris 5 (*General etching supplies*)

City Gate Inks, City Gate Unit, Nobel Road, City Est. London N18 (*Lithographic stones*)

Coates Bros (Inks) Ltd, Easton Street, Rosebery Avenue, London WC1 (*Screen printing ink*)

Coates Bros (Litho Plates) Ltd, Easton Street, Rosebery Avenue, London WC1 (*Lithographic plates*)

Cornelissen & Sons, 22 Great Queen Street, London WC2 (*General lithographic supplies*)

Cowling & Wilcox, 26 Broadwick Street, London W1 (*General art supplies, tools, inks, and knives*)

Cranco Engineering Ltd., Chapel Street, Long Eaton, Nottingham, NG10 1EQ (*Presses, frames, stretching equipment*)

Croda Inks Ltd, Reliance Works, Devonshire Road, SW19 or Park Works, Park Lane, Harefield (*Relief printing ink*)

Curwen Prints Ltd, 9 North Street, E13 (*Editioning of artists' lithographs by offset and direct*)

Dane & Co. Ltd, Sugar House Lane, Stratford, London E15 2QN (*Screen printing ink*)

Essex Printers Supply Co., Elektron Works, Norlington Road, Leyton, London E10 (*Presses*)

Falkiner Fine Papers, 4 Mart Street, Covent Garden, London WC2E 8DE (*Fine papers of all descriptions*)

A. Gallenkamp & Co. Ltd, P.O. Box 290, Technico House, Christopher Street, London EC2P 2ER (*Water jet filter pumps*)

A. R. Gibbon Ltd, 22 Coleman Fields, London N1 7AE (*Lithographic and letterpress ink*)

A. Gilby & Son Ltd, Reliance Works, Devonshire Road, Colliers Wood, London SW19 (*Lithographic and letterpress ink*)

Grafica Ltd, 108a Fulham Road, London W6 (*Offset litho processors*)

Grant Equipment and Supplies, Grant House, Kingston House Estate, Portsmouth Road, Thames Ditton, Surrey (*Process cameras, enlargers, drying cabinets*)

Green's Fine Papers Division, W. & R. Balston Ltd, Springfield Mill, Maidstone, Kent ME14 2LE (*Hand-made and mould-made papers*)

Hall Mark Machine Industries Ltd., Risley, Derby DE7 3SS (*Presses*)

George Hall Ltd, Hardman Street, Chestergate, Stockport, Cheshire (*Presses, equipment, stencil films*)

Horsell Graphic Industries Ltd, Howley Park Estate, Morley, Leeds LS27 0QT (*Printing inks, offset plates, general lithographic supplies*)

Howeson Algraphy, Murray Road, St. Pauls Cray, Orpington, Kent (*Parker exposure units, light boxes*)

Hunter Penrose Littlejohn Ltd, 7 Spa Road, London SE16 3QS (*Presses, rollers, sink units, graphic art and printing supplies, film chemicals, metal plates*)

Ilford Ltd, Christopher Martin Road, Basildon (*Photographic equipment*)

Inveresk Paper Co. Ltd, Clan House, 19 Tudor Street, London EC4Y 0BA (*Hand-made and mould-made paper*)

Kast+Ehinger GmbH, *Printing Inks, 7 Stuttgart-Feuerback, Germany. Represented in United Kingdom by* **National Printing Ink Co. Ltd,** Industrial Estate, Chichester, Sussex (*Printing inks*)

John T. Keep & Sons Ltd, 15 Theobald's Road, London WC1 (*Screen inks*)

H.G. Kippar + Sons Ltd., Upper Bankfield Mills, Almondbury Bank, Huddersfield HD5 8HF

Kodak Ltd., Products Distribution, P.O. Box 33, Swallowdale Road, Hemel Hempstead, Herts. (*Kodatrace, films, developers*)

E. A. Kuffall & Co. Ltd, 157 Dukes Road, London W3 (*Mesh materials*)

T. N. Lawrence, 2-4 Bleeding Heart Yard, Greville Street, Hatton Garden, London EC1 (*Papers, rollers, inks, wood blocks(reground), catalogue*)

Littlejohn Graphic Systems Ltd, 16-24 Brewery Road, London N7 9DP (*Dark room cameras and equipment, graphic art enlargers, contact printing frames, colour reproduction systems*)

E. T. Marler Ltd, Deer Park Road, Wimbledon, London SW19 3UE (*Printing inks, mesh materials, printing tables, mercury vapour lamps, copysacs*)

Modbury Engineering, Belsize Mews, 27 Belsize Lane, London NW3 5AT (*Supply of aquatint boxes, cast iron hot tables for etching, lithographic stones, levigators, rebuilt proof presses; maintenance and repair of etching, lithographic and relief proofing presses*)

Paperchase Products Ltd, 216 Tottenham Court Road, London W1A 3DM (*Paper*)

Papierfabrik Zerkall, Renker & Söhne, D-5161 Zerkall über Düren, Federal Republic of Germany (*Mould-made papers and boards*)

Philips Electrical Ltd, City House, 420-430 London Road, Croydon CR9 3QR (*Mercury vapour lamps*)

A. J. Polak, 439-443 North Circular Road, London NW10 0HR (*Mesh materials*)

Peter Potter Products, Oliver Products Development Ltd., Water Lane, Storrington, Sussex (*General screen printing equipment*)

Pronk, Davis & Rusby Ltd, 90-96 Brewery Road, London N7 9PD (*Mesh materials, general screen printing equipment*)

A. J. Purdy & Co. Ltd, 248 Lea Bridge Road, Leyton, London E10 (*Mesh materials*)

Register Print Machinery Ltd., 360 Brighton Road, South Croydon, Surrey CR2 6AL

Harry F. Rochat, Cotswold Lodge, Stapylton Road, Barnet, Herts (*Supplier of presses, some secondhand*)

Rowney & Co. Ltd., 12 Percy Street, London W1 (*Inks, tools, blocks, paper and general supplies*)

Samco-Strong Ltd, P.O. Box 88, Clay Hill, Bristol BS99 7ER (*Screen printing tables and other equipment*)

Sansom Bros Ltd, 1a McDermott Road, London SE15 (*Lithographic plates and regrainers*)

Charles Schmautz, 219 Rue Raymond Losserand, 75 Paris 14 (*General lithographic supplies*)

The S.D. Syndicate Ltd, 121 Westminster Bridge Road, London SE1 7HR (*Photo engraving copper and zinc sheets and associated chemicals*)

Selactasine Silk Screens Ltd, 22 Bulstrode Street, London W1M 5FR. Mail order, 65 Chislehurst Road, Chislehurst, Kent (*Mesh materials and printing tables*)

Sericol Group Ltd, 24 Parsons Green Lane, London SW6 4HS (*Screen printing inks, mesh materials, mercury vapour lamps, copysacs, autotype materials*)

Serigraphics, Fairfield Avenue, Maesteg, Glam., Wales (*Screen printing equipment and materials*)

Spicer-Cowan Ltd, New Hythe House, Aylesford, Maidstone, Kent ME20 7PD (*Paper*)

Alec Tiranti Ltd, 72 Charlotte Street, London W1 (*Engraving tools*)

Usher-Walker Ltd, Chancery House, Chancery Lane, London WC2 (*Copperplate inks*)

Winsor & Newton, 5 Rathbone Place, London W2 (*Inks, tools, blocks, papers and general supplies*)

Winstones Ltd, Park Works, Park Lane, Harefield (*Printing inks and rollers*)

Wiggins Teape Ltd, Belgrave House, Basing View, Basingstoke RG21 2EE (*Printing papers*)

AMERICAN SUPPLIERS

American Screen Process Equipment Company, 1439 West Hubbard Street, Chicago 22, Ill. (*Presses and general screen printing supplies*)

Andrews, Nelson, Whitehead, Boise Cascade Corporation, 7 Laight Street, New York, NY 10013 (*Paper*)

Apex Roller Company, 1541 North 16th Street, St Louis, Missouri 63106 (*Rollers*)

Becker Sign Supply Company, 319-321 North Paca Street, Baltimore 1, Md. (*General screen printing supplies*)

Charles Brand Machinery Inc., 84 East 10th Street, New York, NY 10003 (*Etching and lithographic presses, rollers, hot plates, general supplies*)

Challenge Machinery Company, Grand Haven, Michigan 49417 (*General equipment*)

Cincinnati Screen Process Supplies, Inc., 1111 Meta Drive Cincinnati 37, Ohio (*Drying ovens and related supplies*)

Craftool Inc., 1 Industrial Avenue, Woodridge, New Jersey 07075 (*Woodcarving and cutting tools*)

The Craftool Company, 1421 West 240th Street, Harbor City, California 90710 (*Woodcarving and cutting tools*)

B. Drakenfeld & Company, 45-47 Park Place, New York 7, NY (*Screen fabrics, ceramic colors, decal papers*)

E. I. Du Pont de Nemours & Company, Inc., 2410-17 Nemours Building, Washington 98, Del. (*Photographic equipment*)

Eastman Kodak Company, Rochester 4, NY (*Photographic equipment*)

Graphic Chemical & Ink Company, 728 North Yale Avenue, Villa Park, Ill. 60181 (*Ink and presses*)

Graphic Equipment of Boston, Inc., 22 Simmons Street, Boston 20, Mass. (*Presses and related equipment*)

Ideal and Graphic Rollers Company, 30 31st Street, Long Island City, NY 11102 (*Rollers*)

Interchemical Printing Ink Corporation, 67 West 44 Street, New York, NY (*Printing inks*)

Japan Paper Company, 7 Laight Street, New York, NY 10013 (*Paper*)

W. M. Korn, Inc., 260 West Street, New York, NY 10013 (*Lithographic and silk screen crayons, general lithographic supplies*)

Lawson Printing Machine company, 4453 Olive Street, St Louis 8, Missouri (*Printing equipment*)

McLogan's Screen Process Supply House, 1324 South Hope Street, Los Angeles 15, Calif.

M. & M. Research Engineering Company, 13360 West Silver Spring Road, Butler, Wisconsin (*Presses and related equipment*)

Edward C. Muller, 3646 White Plains Road, Bronx, New York, 10467 (*Woodcarving and cutting tools*)

Nu-Arc Company, Inc., 4110 West Grand Avenue, Chicago 51, Ill. (*Photographic equipment*)

Printing Aids Corporation, 9333 King Street, Franklin Park, Chicago, Ill. (*Printing consultants and equipment*)

Roberts & Porter Inc., 4140 West Victoria Avenue, Chicago, Ill. 60646 (*Ink, rollers, blankets, general supplies*)

Tamerind Institute, 108 Cornell Avenue, SE, Albuquerque, New Mexico 87106 (*Lithographic printing services*)

Zellerback Paper Company, 245 South Spruce Avenue, San Francisco, Calif. 94118

INDEX

Acknowledgments

The publishers would like to thank the following people for their kind help and assistance:
Ken Stubbs and Frank Tinsley for special photography and the Principal, staff and students of Camberwell School of Art, London.
Robin Bagilhole, 'and Printmaking' exhibition, Waterloo Gallery, London.
Pronk, Davis, Rusby Ltd.
Trumax Ltd.
Lesley Thomas
Atlantis Paper Company for supplying paper
St. Martins School of Art, London.
All the artists/printmakers who lent their work.
Stanley Jones of Curwen Press.

All pictures by Ken Stubbs except: 'and Printmaking' exhibition 7, 11, 14, 42, 49, 60, 74-75, 90, 94, 99, 107. Laurence Bradbury 37, 70-71, 97, 108. Chris Holiday 37. Francis Lumley 15, 78, 79, 106. Pronk, Davis, Rusby 98. Thumb Gallery, London 90, 91, 95. Line drawings by Smith Brown Partnership except 105, by Trumax Ltd, Bristol. The Woodcuts on pages 76, 83 are reproduced by kind permission of Minale Tattersfield Ltd and Boots. Front cover: Laurence Bradbury, Ken Stubbs. Back cover: Print by Claire Pollock. Project devised by Robin Bagilhole and Neal Bassant at St. Martins School of Art, London.